The
LAND
of the
GODS

ALSO BY H. P. BLAVATSKY

The Secret Doctrine

Isis Unveiled

The Key to Theosophy

The Voice of the Silence

From the Caves and Jungles of Hindostan

The People of the Blue Mountains

The Durbar in Lahore

Collected Writings

H. P. BLAVATSKY

The
LAND
of the
GODS

The Long-Hidden Story of Visiting the Masters of Wisdom in Shambhala

Radiant Books
New York

The Land of the Gods was first published anonymously in 1887 as *An Adventure Among the Rosicrucians* under the pseudonym "A Student of Occultism." It was republished in 1910 as *With the Adepts* under the name of Franz Hartmann, who acknowledged that he was not its original author.

Copy-edited by Sandy Draper. Cover and interior illustrations by Kateryna Velcheva.

Illustrations © 2022 by Radiant Books
Glossary © 2022 by Radiant Books

Library of Congress Control Number: 2022945434

Published in 2022 by Radiant Books
radiantbooks.co

ISBN 978-1-63994-025-7 (hardback)
ISBN 978-1-63994-024-0 (paperback)
ISBN 978-1-63994-023-3 (e-book)

CONTENTS

PUBLISHER'S NOTE

This book was originally published anonymously by a mysterious "Student of Occultism" in 1887 under the title *An Adventure Among the Rosicrucians*, yet with copyright in the name of Franz Hartmann. Helena Blavatsky reviewed it, describing it as: "A strange and original little story, charmingly fantastic, but full of poetic feeling and, what is more, of deep philosophical and occult truths, for those who can perceive the groundwork it is built upon."[1]

In 1910, Hartmann republished the story titled *With the Adepts* along with new additions, as well as omissions. However, in his preface, he mentioned that it "has been gathered from notes handed to me by a friend, a writer of considerable repute."[2]

Those notes were originally written by H. P. Blavatsky because only she could gain access to the Holy of Holies on the Earth — the secret Abode of the Masters of Wisdom, known as Shambhala. In 1939, Helena Roerich, who continued Blavatsky's mission in the 20th century, also confirmed her authorship: "This account of the inner life of the Brotherhood was undoubtedly recorded by Franz Hartmann from the words of H. P. Blavatsky, conveyed with some changes in literary form."[3]

The Chief Stronghold of Shambhala is located in the heart of the Himalayas. However, the network of its Abodes is also spread within other mountainous and remote locations around the world, in the most inaccessible places. The notes that Madame Blavatsky prepared were, in fact, different stories that occurred both in the Himalayas and the Alps at various times, yet were later tied into one single story narrating the secret order of the Rosicrucians.

---

[1] H. P. Blavatsky, "An Adventure Among the Rosicrucians," *Collected Writings*, vol. 8 (Wheaton, IL: Theosophical Publishing House, 1966), p. 130.

[2] Franz Hartmann, *With the Adepts* (New York: Theosophical Publishing Co, 1910), p. v.

[3] Helena Roerich, *Pis'ma* [Letters], vol. 6 (Moscow: Mezhdunarodnyi tsentr Rerikhov, 2006), p. 513.

The publisher hopes that one day it will be permitted to tell more about this book and its characters, as it was originally intended since the discovery of Blavatsky's work was made in June 2015 — a work that she hid in plain sight long ago.

The new edition, now published for the first time under the name of its true author, is primarily based on the 1887 original yet also contains additions from the 1910 edition. However, several things that Helena Blavatsky allowed Franz Hartmann to add to make her story his have been eliminated, and the chapter titles have been changed. The text has also been edited according to modern linguistic standards to make it more appropriate for 21st-century readers.

Dedicated to Sophia,
the Divine Mother of
Faith, Hope, and Love.

I

THE BEAUTY
OF THE
MOUNTAINS

I am penning these lines in a little village in the Alpine mountains in Southern Bavaria, only a short distance from the Austrian frontier. The impressions I received yesterday are still fresh in my mind; the experiences which caused them were as real to me as any other driven by the events of everyday life. Nevertheless, they were of such an extraordinary character that I can't persuade myself that they were more than a dream.

Having finished the long and tedious labour of investigating the Rosicrucians' history and studying old worm-eaten books, mouldy manuscripts hardly legible from age, passing days and parts of night in convent libraries and antiquarian shops, collecting and copying everything that seemed of any value for my object in view, I made up my mind to grant myself a few days' holiday among the sublime scenery of the Tyrolian Alps.

The mountains were still covered in snow, although the spring had advanced. But I was anxious to escape the city's turmoil and noise, to breathe once more the pure, exhilarating air of the mountain heights, to see the shining glaciers glistening like vast mirrors in the light of the rising sun, and to share the feeling of the poet Byron when he wrote the following verses:

He who ascends to mountain tops shall find
The loftiest peaks most wrapp'd in clouds and snow;
He who surpasses or subdues mankind
Must look down on the hate of those below;
Though high above the sun of glory glow,
And far beneath the earth and ocean spread,
Round him are icy rocks, and loudly blow
Contending tempests on his naked head,
And thus reward the toils which to these summits led.

Boarding the train at K., I soon arrived at S. Thence, I wandered on foot, highly enjoying the change from the smoky atmosphere of the crowded streets to the fresh air of the country, pregnant with the odour of pines and daisies, the latter appearing where the snow had gone. The road led up through the river valley, and, as I advanced, the valley grew narrower and the sides of the mountain steeper. Here and there were clusters of farmhouses and some rustic cottages clinging to the projecting rocks of the mountains as if seeking protection against the storms which often blow through these valleys. The sun was sinking down below the western horizon and gilded the snowy peaks of the mountains and the brazen cross on the top of the spire of the little village church, from which tolled the curfew, or, as it is here called, the *Ave Maria* when I arrived at O., — the starting point for my excursions into the mountains.

Finding a hospitable reception in the village inn, I soon retired and awoke early in the morning, having been aroused from my sleep by the tinkling of little bells hanging around the necks of the goats sent out to their pasturage. I arose and stepped to the window. The night's shadows were fleeing before the approach of the coming sun; the dawn had begun, and before me in sublime array stood the grand old peaks of the mountains, reminding me of Edwin Arnold's description of the view from the windows of Prince Siddhartha's palace, Vishramvan. There the grand mountains stood:

> *Ranged in white ranks against the blue-untrod*
> *Infinite, wonderful — whose uplands vast,*
> *And lifted universe of crest and crag,*
> *Shoulder and shelf, green slope and icy horn,*
> *Riven ravine and splintered precipice,*
> *Led climbing thought higher and higher, until*
> *It seemed to stand in heaven and speak with gods.*

Soon I was on the way and wandered farther up through the valley along the riverbed, but here it was merely a small stream, rushing and dancing wildly over the rocks, while farther down, where it had grown, it flowed in tranquil majesty through the plains. The valley seemed to cut through long mountain ranges, and other valleys opened into this. Some of these valleys were known to me as I had roamed them and explored their mysterious recesses, caves, and forests some twenty years ago. Still, there was one mysterious valley I hadn't yet explored, which led towards a high, bifurcated mountain peak, whose summit was said to be inaccessible, and upon which the foot of no mortal had ever trod. Towards this valley, I seemed to be attracted by some invisible but irresistible power. I felt as if, in its unexplored depths at the foot of this inaccessible mountain, the secret and undefined longings of my heart were to be satisfied, as if a mystery would be revealed to me whose solution couldn't be found in books.

The sun hadn't yet risen, and the dark woods to the right and left were of a uniform colour. As I entered the narrow, mysterious valley, the path rose gradually, leading through a dark forest along the side of a mountain. Slowly and almost imperceptibly, it ascended. At first, it was near the rushing stream, but as I progressed, the torrent's roar sounded more distant; the foaming stream seemed to sink farther down. At last, the forest became thinner, and the dark woods were now far below me; before me and above the intervening trees rose the naked cliffs of the inaccessible mountain. Still, the path led up higher. Soon the distant noise of a waterfall was heard, and I approached again the bed of the mountain stream, which now seemed to be a mass of rocks, split into pieces by some giant power, lying about in wild confusion, while the white foam of the water danced between the cliffs.

Here and there were little islands of soil covered with green vegetation. They stood like isolated tables amid the wilderness; for the combined action of water and air had decomposed and eaten away a great part of their foundations, and they looked like plates of soil resting upon small pedestals; hard as they are, their final tumble is merely a question of time, for their foundations were slowly crumbling away.

My path took me upwards, sometimes nearing the riverbed, sometimes receding from it, sometimes over steep rocks, and again descending to the bottom of ravines formed by the melting snow. Thus I entered deep into the mysterious valley when the first signs of sunrise appeared upon the cliffs above my head. One of these towering peaks was crowned with a halo of light, while beyond it, the full sunlight streamed into the valley below. A mild breeze swept through the treetops, and the foliage of the birch trees, with which the pine forest was sprinkled, trembled in the morning air. No sound could now be heard, except occasionally the note of a titmouse, and more rarely the cry of a hawk which rose in long-drawn, spiral motions high up into the air to begin its day's work.

Now the ash-grey walls and cliffs began to assume a pale silvery hue, while in the rents and crags of the rock, the dark blue shade seemed to resist the influence of the light. Looking backwards, I saw how the valley widened, and, far down, the stream could be seen wandering towards the plains. Obtaining more room as it advanced, it spread and formed ponds and tanks and little lakes among the meadows. On the opposite side of the valley, the tops of high mountains rose far into the sky, and between the interstices of the summits, still more summits arose. The foot of the range was covered with dark vegetation, but the mountainsides exhibited a great variety of colours, from the almost black appearance of the rocks below to the ethereal white of the farthest peaks, whose delicate hues seemed to blend with the pale blue sky. Here and there, the surface was already covered with spots of light from the rising sun, falling through the rents of the rocks and through the branches of trees, foreboding the near arrival of the orb of day. Thus the higher peaks enjoyed the warm sunlight long before it shone into the valley below, but while it shone in its full brightness upon the mountaintops, the dark shadows in the deep valley became thinner and began to disappear.

At last, the solemn moment arrived, and the sun rose in sublime majesty over the mountaintops, becoming visible to all. The shadows fled, and a flood of light penetrated the valley, lighting up the dark pine forest and illuminating the rock caves. Shining upon the fields of snow and the glaciers, its light was reflected as in a mirror and produced a blinding effect, but upon the rocky surface, it softened, giving it the appearance of a thousand various hues.

The road turned round a projecting part of the mountain height, and suddenly I stood in full view of the inaccessible mountain. Between where I stood and the base of the mountain, there was a well-nigh treeless plain, and the soil was almost without vegetation. Everywhere the ground was covered with stones and rocks, many of which seemed to have fallen down from the mysterious mountain and broken in the fall. Here and there was a small spot covered with moss or thin vegetation, sending fantastically shaped green branches upwards along the sides of the inaccessible mountain towards the bare grey walls of the summit, where giant sentinels of a forbidding mien stood eternal and immovable, and seemed to defend their strongholds against the aggressive vegetation, crowding the latter back into the valley. Thus the everlasting combat raging for untold ages still continued, but the frontlines of the contending armies changed from year to year. Everlasting, like the eternal truths, stand the bare grey rocks upon the summits; here and there, the vegetation invades their kingdom, like illusions approaching the realm of the real; death is victorious; the green spots are buried each year under the descending rocks; but again life is the victor, for those rocks decay, and a new life appears upon their withered faces.

In the limestone formation of the Alpine ranges, the rocks decomposed by wind and rain often assume the most fantastic shapes, which suggest the names given to the mountains. Very little imagination is required to behold the shape in the summits of the Wilden Kaiser mountain, the figure of the Emperor Barbarossa, with his long red beard, crown and sceptre, lying in state, unaffected by the cold of the winter or the summer's heat, waiting to be resurrected; or we may see in the shape of the Hochvogel the form of an eagle spreading its wings; in the Widder-horn, the shape of the horns of a ram, etc. At the base of the mountains and valleys, the soil is covered with small loose rocks and piles of sand, in the midst of which coltsfoot spreads its large green leaves, and the blue bell-shaped flowers of monkshood wave their heads. In some secluded spots grows the celebrated edelweiss, resembling in size those which grow on the Popocatepetl in Mexico and the Cordilleras of South America. There may also be found the mountain gentian, the Alpine rose, the mandrake, mountain arnica, the mysterious St. John's wort, and other curious plants full of healing powers and strange virtues. Wherever a sufficient quantity of soil has accumulated to enable a tree to grow, a larger kind of vegetation appears. Still, the little crust of earth isn't deep enough to afford a solid footing for large trees. They may grow to a certain height, but someday a storm will arise and sweep down the mountainsides, and then the work of destruction begins. Grand old tree corpses, whose roots have been torn from the soil, lie about, their barkless, bleached branches like so many skeleton arms stretched up towards heaven as if they had been calling for help in the hour of their death, but no help had arrived. Smaller growths of dwarf trees surround them and cover the ground or feed like parasites upon the substance of the dead.

The spring had advanced, but among these mountains, the seasons are interlaced with each other. The red and yellow leaves painted by autumn are seen among the green foliage of the stunted pines. The moss clinging to the steep precipices shows the reddish colour of autumn, and in many clefts and caverns linger the snow and ice of the past winter. Still, above the red and green and the pure white snow, the grey masses of the summits rise in a succession of pillars and points, with domes and spires and pinnacles, like a city built by the gods, while in the background spreads the grey or blue canopy of heaven. Thin streams of water run down from these heights over the precipices, and as they splash over the projecting rocks, they are reduced to vapour before reaching the ground below. The rocks themselves have been hollowed out, forming large caves, indicating how powerful those little veins of water may become if swelled by the floods from the melting snows of the summits.

After enjoying the sublime scenery for a few minutes, I continued on my way and approached a little stream from a waterfall in the distance. I wandered along its border; the water was deep but so clear that even the smallest pebble could be distinctly seen at the bottom. Sometimes it appeared as motionless as if it were liquid crystal penetrated by the sun's rays, and again, meeting obstacles in its way, it foamed in its rocky bed as if in a sudden fit of rage. While in other places, the water tumbled in little cascades over pretty pebbles and stones, forming miniature cataracts which exhibited various colours.

In this solitude, there is nothing to remind one of humanity's existence except the occasional sawn-off tree trunk, showing the destructive influence of human activity. Rainwater collected in some old, rotten, hollow trunks sparkled in the sun like little mirrors, such as may be used by water nymphs. Around their edges, little mushrooms are growing, which our imagination transforms into chairs, tables, and baldachinos for fairies and elves.

Where I stood, the ground was covered with moss, with the occasional great, white thistle, whose sharp-pointed leaves sparkled in the sunlight. At a short distance, I saw a small grove of pines, looking like an island in the desert, and to that grove, I directed my steps. There I resolved to rest and enjoy the beauty of Nature. I laid myself down upon the moss in a place overshadowed by a mighty pine. The music of the mountain stream was heard at a distance, and opposite to where I rested, there was a waterfall, spreading into a vapour as it fell over the rocks, and in the haze appeared the colours of the rainbow. The mist fell into a basin formed of rock, and from a rent in this basin, overgrown with moss, the water foamed and rushed, hastening down towards the valley to become united with the main body of the river.

For a long time, I watched the water play, and the longer I watched, the more it became alive with forms of the most singular shape. Supermundane beings of great beauty seemed to dance in the spray, shaking their heads in the sunshine and throwing showers of liquid silver from their streaming curls and waving locks. Their laughter sounded like that of the falls of Minnehaha, and from the rock crevices peeped the ugly faces of gnomes and kobolds slyly watching the fairies dance. Above the fall, the current seemed to hesitate before throwing itself over the precipice; but below, where it left the basin, it appeared to be irritated by the impediments in its way and impatient to leave its home; while far down in the valley, where it became united to its brother, the river, it sounded as if the latter was welcoming it back to its bosom, and as if both were exulting over their final union in a glad jubilee.

What is the reason that we imagine such things? Why do we endow "dead things" with human consciousness and sensation? Why are we, in our moments of happiness, unsatisfied to feel that we live in a body, but our consciousness craves to go out of its prison-house and mix with the universal life? Is our consciousness merely a product of the organic activity of our physical body, or is it a function of the universal life, concentrated — so to say — in focus within the physical body? Is our personal consciousness dependent for its existence on the physical body, and does it die with the latter; or is there a spiritual consciousness belonging to a higher, immortal, and invisible spiritual self, which is temporarily connected with the physical organism, but which may exist independently of the latter? If such is the case, if our physical organism is merely an instrument through which our consciousness acts, then this instrument is not our real self. If this is true, our real self is where our consciousness exists and may exist independently of the latter. If we mentally float along the curves of the mountaintops, sinking gradually downwards, rising suddenly upwards, and examining in our imagination the things upon their surface, why do we feel such a sense of exhilaration and joy, as if we were really there, but had to leave our material body behind because it is too heavy to accompany the spirit to the top of the inaccessible mountain? Is it true that a part of our life and consciousness must remain in its physical form to enable it to continue to live during our absence and to attend to the functions of life? Still, we have read of somnambules and persons in an ecstatic condition whose inner spiritual self — with all its powers of consciousness, sensation, and perception — was absent from their apparently dead forms and who visited distant places, going and returning with the velocity of thought, and bringing descriptions of such places which were afterwards verified and found to be true.

Why do we find life in all things, even those considered "dead," if we merely put ourselves in a condition where we can perceive that they are living? Can there be any dead matter in the Universe? Is not even a stone held together by the "cohesion" of its particles and attracted to the Earth by "gravitation"? But what else is this "cohesion" and "gravitation" but energy, and what is "energy" but the soul, an interior principle called *force*, which produces an outward manifestation called *matter*; but which must ultimately be identical with force or substance, or by whatever name we may call a thing of which we have no conception. If this view is correct, all things possess life, all things possess soul, and there may be soul-beings whose outward forms are not so gross as ours and who are therefore invisible to our physical senses but may be perceived by our own soul.

In the silence of Nature, thoughts grow to be waking dreams, and dreams become visions. I imagined how in this solemn solitude I might remain for the rest of my life, perhaps sharing my habitation with a few congenial friends. I imagined how, united by common interests and having identical objects in view, we might be happy and obtain knowledge together. Here, far away from the superficiality and shallowness of common life, a far greater clearness of mental perception, a much deeper concentration of thought, and a much higher conception of the truth regarding the mysteries of Nature and human beings might be obtained. How much would our senses be sharpened to perceive external and internal things? How much would our knowledge of self increase? What should we care about the tomfooleries of what is called *society*? What should we care to know about what is going on in that great insane asylum called *the world*? Here we could live undisturbed within our own selves, unpestered by the necromantic practices of "society," which daily and hourly force us to go out from our selves, to appear where we don't desire to be, compel us to act as we don't desire to act, to bow down before the goddess of fashion, whom we despise in our hearts.

Would such a life be useful for us and useful for others? If it is true that the world and we are made up of ideas, then it is just in such solitudes that the best conditions might be found to grasp and remodel ideas. Thoughts and ideas can't be mere illusions; they must have a real existence, as real and perhaps more lasting than the objective things of this world, for we know that ideas outlive the death of the forms in which they are represented. We know that

ideas, like other fruits, are born and become mature, and whenever
an idea is mature, it appears on the mental horizon of the world
and is often grasped at the same time by some receptive minds.
One who can grasp and remodel exalted ideas, and give them material expression, may do much more for the world's benefit by
living alone and in solitude than by living among the world where
their work is continually impeded by affairs of minor importance.
The ideas which they shape won't die with their body. They will be
thrown upon the great mirror, the Astral Light, and be preserved
in the world's memory to be grasped and utilized by others.

What is that being we call *human*, after all? What is this living animal organism of flesh, blood, and bones, nerves and mind,
which lives for a while and then dies, and which the great majority
of people esteem so highly, as if it were their own immortal self,
and for the comfort of which they often sacrifice their self-respect,
their dignity, honour, and virtue? Is it anything else than an animal
in whom an intellectual activity of a higher order than in other
animals predominates? Can this mental activity be the product
of the mechanical, chemical, and physiological activity of dead
matter? If not, what is the cause of this activity, and can this cause
exist independently of the form? What is a human being without
any intelligence? If intelligence, as it must be, is an attribute of
the spirit, what is a human being without any spirit and without
spiritual intelligence?

While meditating on this question, a stupid laugh sounded
close by my side. I had been so engaged with my thoughts that I
hadn't noticed the stranger's approach, but looking up, I saw close
by my side one of those locals often found in the mountainous
countries of Switzerland and Savoy. I was somewhat surprised and
startled and not a little annoyed at the unwelcome interruption,
and I asked him rather abruptly, "What do you want?"

A broad grin passed over the dwarf's face, for such he certainly
was, as he answered, "Master says I should guide you to his house."
I was somewhat astonished by his reply, but thinking that no intelligent answer was to be expected from him, I asked, "Who is
your master?" His answer was, "Imperator," and as he spoke that

word, a spark of intelligence seemed to shine in his eyes, and his tone indicated that this Imperator, whoever he might be, was undoubtedly somebody to whom this dwarf rendered implicit obedience. I attempted to ask him more questions and find out who this Imperator was or where he lived, but all my efforts were to no avail, and the dwarf merely grinned and repeated the words he had already said. Therefore, I finally decided to go with him and see how the adventure would end.

The dwarf walked ahead, and I followed him towards the base of the inaccessible mountain. While walking, my guide often turned back to see whether I was following him, so I had a good opportunity to study his dress and features. He wasn't over three feet high and evidently a hunchback. His clothing consisted of a hooded brown gown, which made him appear like a small Capuchin monk of the order of St. Augustine. An immense big head and a comparatively large body rested upon very thin and small legs, while his feet seemed again to be extraordinarily large. Perhaps because of his small size and the healthy colour of his face, he appeared to be almost a child; but this opinion was contradicted by the grey beard of considerable length adorning his face. He carried a staff made of a tree limb, which he had evidently picked up on his way.

II

MEETING
THE LORD OF
SHAMBHALA

I followed my companion, and soon we regained the path running along the bed of the creek, which flowed tranquilly over the white pebbles, and the shallowness of the water indicated that we were not far from its source. As we approached the mysterious mountain, the stone walls appeared to rise perpendicularly before us, and there was no place visible where any other being but a bird could have ascended. However, as we came nearer, I noticed a rent or break in the side of the wall, opening like a cave or a tunnel. This tunnel we entered, and I saw that it penetrated the giant wall and led into another valley beyond. A few steps brought us to the other end of the tunnel, and an exclamation of joy and surprise escaped my lips as I beheld a beautiful sight.

Before me was a valley surrounded by mountains of evidently inaccessible height, where Nature and art seemed to have combined to endow it with an almost superterrestrial beauty. Like a vast ocean bay, it opened before my sight, closing in the distance with a natural amphitheatre. It was covered with short grass and planted with maple trees, and on all sides, there were forests and groves, small lakes and lovely creeks. Immediately in front of me, but still at a considerable distance, rose the vault of a sublime mountain peak high into the blue ether of space, presenting a cavity with overhanging rocks, looking like the hollow space under a gigantic wave, which had been petrified by some magic spell. The sides of the mountain sank in energetically drawn lines towards a lower declivity and then rose abruptly to an imposing height.

In the presence of so much sublimity, I became silent, awestruck. My companion seemed to comprehend my feeling, for he, too, stood still and laughed as if pleased to see how full of admiration I was. The surrounding stillness would have been complete if it had not been for the noise of a cataract, at a distance to the left, falling over a steep precipice and appearing like a string of fluid silver backed by the dark grey rock. The monotonous rush of that fall in contradistinction to the surrounding stillness seemed like the rush of the river of time in the realm of eternity; another world than the one to which I was accustomed seemed to have descended upon me; the air seemed purer, the light more ethereal, the grass greener than on the other side of the tunnel; here seemed to be the valley of peace, the paradise of happiness and content.

Looking towards the high peak in the distance, I noticed what seemed to be a palace, a fortress, or a monastery of some kind, and as I came nearer, I saw it was a massive stone building. Its high walls rose above the surrounding treetops, and a dome, like a temple, crowned the top of the building. Its exterior appearance indicated the solidity of the walls. It was built in rectangular form, but its architecture wasn't of a regular style; it presented many projecting windows, turrets, balconies, and verandas.

On the other side of the valley, Nature wasn't less sublime and inspiring. Grey giant cliffs, standing out prominently against the steel-blue background of the sky, rose up to an extraordinary height. Below the highest peaks, long strips of white clouds had settled around the mountain and seemed to separate the top of the latter from its main body. The part below the cloud was partly covered by the shadow and partly illuminated by a pale ghostly light, producing a glamour. There, where the masses of clouds rested against the bulk of the mountain, it seemed that I was looking into a world of destruction. It was as if the mountain's entrails had been torn up, and the uniformity of the desolate jumble of rocks was only interrupted by a few remnants of snow situated in the caverns and on the crags of the mountain.

As we advanced, we came into a broad avenue leading to the building, and I beheld a man of noble and imposing appearance approaching. He was clad in a yellow robe, his head covered with black flowing hair, and he walked with an elastic step. When my guide saw this man, he hurried towards him, prostrated himself before him, and suddenly vanished like an image from a dream.

I was astonished by this extraordinary occurrence but didn't have time to reflect, for the stranger approached me and bid me welcome. He appeared to be about thirty-five years of age, of tall and commanding stature, and his mild and benevolent look, full of spiritual energy, seemed to penetrate my whole being and to read my innermost thoughts. "Surely," I thought, "this man is an Adept!"

"Yes," answered the stranger, as if reading my thoughts, "you have fallen into the hands of the Adepts, of whom you have thought so much and whose acquaintance you often desired to make, and I will introduce you into our temple and make you acquainted with some of our *Brothers of the Golden and Rosy Cross.*"

I scanned his face, and now it seemed this man wasn't a stranger. There was something so familiar about him as if I had known him for years, yet I couldn't place him in my memory. In vain, I tortured my brain to find out when or where I had met this man, or at least someone resembling him. But again, the Imperator of this "Rosicrucian Society," for such he proved to be, answered my unspoken thought by saying: "You are right; we are not strangers, for I have often been in your presence and stood by your side, although you didn't see me. I have directed the flow of ideas which streamed into your brain while you elaborated on them and put them down in writing. Moreover, you have often visited this place while your physical body was sleeping, and you have conversed with the Brothers and me. Still, when your soul returned to its house of flesh and blood, it couldn't impress the memory of the brain with the recollection of the events through which you had passed, and you could remember none of your transcendental experiences when you awoke. The memory of the material form retains only the impressions made upon it by the avenues of the external senses; the memory of the spirit awakens when we are in the spiritual state."

I told the Imperator that I considered this day the happiest in my life and only regretted that I shouldn't be permitted to remain here forever, as I felt that I wasn't yet worthy of remaining in the society of beings so far exalted above my own state.

"We shall not permit you to go away very soon," answered the Master. "You will have ample time to see how we live. But as to your permanently remaining here, this is at present an impossibility. You have other duties to perform, and, moreover, there are still too many of the lower and animal elements adhering to your constitution and forming a part of yourself. They couldn't resist long the destructive influence of the pure and spiritual air of this place; and as you haven't yet a sufficient amount of truly spiritual elements in your organism to render it firm and strong, you would, by remaining here, soon become weak and waste away like a person in a state of consumption. You would become miserable instead of happy. You would die."

"Master," I said, "then can I at least hope to learn, while I am here, the mystery of those great spiritual powers which you possess, by which you are said to be able to transform one thing into another and transmute base metals into gold?"

"There is nothing mysterious or wonderful about it, my friend," said the Imperator. "Such things are not more wonderful than the ordinary phenomena of Nature which we see every day. They are only mysterious to those whose own prejudices and misconceptions hinder them from seeing the truth and knowing the power the spirit possesses to subjugate matter through the soul. We need not be surprised about them more than seeing the moon revolve around the Earth or watching the growth of a tree. It is all merely the effect of that one primordial power called *the Will* that brought the world into existence. It manifests itself in various ways, and on the seven different planes of existence, as a mechanical force or as a spiritual power; but it is always the same divine primordial power of Will, acting through the instrumentality of the organism of human beings, who direct it by their intelligence."

"Then," I said, "the principal requirement would be to learn how to strengthen the Will?"

"Not so," said the Imperator. "The Will is the *Law*, the universal power holding together the worlds in space and causing the revolutions of planets; it pervades and penetrates everything and doesn't require your strengthening it, for it is already strong enough to accomplish everything possible. You are only an instrument through which this universal power may act and manifest, and you may experience the fullest extent of its strength if you don't attempt to oppose it. But if you imagine you have a *will of your own* whose mode of action differs from the universal will, you merely pervert an insignificant part of the latter and oppose it to the great original power. The more you imagine having such a will of your own, the more you will come into conflict with the original will-power of the Universe. As you are only an insignificant part of the latter, you will be overwhelmed and bring on your own destruction. Your will can only act powerfully if it remains identical to the Will of the Universal Spirit. Your will is strongest if you have no will of your own, but remain in all things obedient to the Law."

"Then," I said, "how can we accomplish anything? If we can do nothing through the power of our own will, we may as well never attempt to do anything but wait until Nature performs her work without our aid."

"We can accomplish nothing useful," answered the Master, "by attempting to employ any separate will of our own; but we may employ our Reason and Intelligence to guide and conduct the already existing universal Will-power in Nature which constitutes the life of all things, and thus we may accomplish in a few moments certain things which it would require unconscious Nature much longer periods to accomplish without our aid. The miller who employs the water of a river to set the mill in motion doesn't create water nor attempts to make the river run upwards towards its source; the miller merely leads the stream into certain channels and intelligently uses the existing current to accomplish their purpose. Knowing the law of Nature, they act in accordance with it. Being obedient to that law, the miller can employ it. Nature obeys those who act in obedience to her laws. In the same manner, act the Adepts. They guide the existing spiritual power by their intelligence and thereby cause it to accomplish certain things in accordance with the law of Nature. Human Intelligence is perhaps the only thing which we may properly call our own, and the highest intelligence to which we may possibly aspire is the perception and understanding of the universal truth.

"Do you see yonder cloud which has settled below the mountaintop?" continued the Adept. "It will remain there until some current of air blows it away or until a change of temperature causes it to rise or to fall. If we disperse it by causing the universal forces of Nature to act upon the dense masses, we don't act against the law of Nature but guide it by our intelligence."

While the Master spoke these words, he extended his hands towards the mountaintop below, where clouds had collected, and immediately it seemed as if life had been infused into the dense mass. It began to whirl and to dance and finally rose like a column of smoke to the top of the mountain, ascending from there high up into the air, giving the mountain the appearance of a volcano. At last, it collected again far above the top, in the air, forming a little silvery cloud through which the sunshine streamed.

I wondered at this manifestation of life in a cloud, but the Adept, reading my thoughts, said: "Life is universal and everywhere; it is identical to the Will. It is not a product of human beings, nor can it be monopolized by them. They receive a certain amount of it when they enter the world; Nature supplies them with it and lends it to them, and they must return it to her again when they *exit* the world. Only one that has succeeded in *fixing* a certain amount of the life-principle within their permanent inner self may call that life their own and retain it after their physical death."

During our conversation, we slowly approached the building, and I had an opportunity to examine its exterior in all its details. It was only two storeys high, but the rooms seemed lofty. It was built in a quadrangular form and surrounded by oaks and maple trees and a large garden or park. Seven steps of white marble led up to the main portal, which was protected by two massive pillars of granite, and over the door appeared in golden letters an inscription, saying: *You, who enter here, leave all evil thoughts behind.*

We entered through the portal into a large vestibule paved with flagstones. Amid this room was a statue of Gautama Buddha on a pedestal, and the walls were ornamented with golden inscriptions representing some of the most important doctrines of the ancient sages. To the right and left, doors opened into long corridors leading to the various apartments of the Brothers. The door opposite the entrance led into a beautiful garden, where I beheld many plants and trees usually only found in tropical climes. The back of the garden was formed by a building of white marble, surrounded by the dome I had seen from a distance after entering the tunnel, and on the top of the dome was a silver dragon resting on a golden globe.

"This," said the Imperator, "is the sanctuary of our temple; in this, you cannot enter. If you were to attempt it, the immediate death of your personality would be the consequence; nor would it serve you even if you were able to enter and live, for, in that sanctuary, everything is dark to all who don't bring with them their own spiritual light, the inextinguishable lamp of divine intelligence, to illuminate the darkness."

We walked into one of the corridors. On our left were numerous doors leading to the Brothers' cells or apartments, but to the right was a wall, occasionally opening into the tropical garden. The interstices between these openings were filled with beautifully painted landscapes. One of these landscapes represented an Indian scene, with the white snow-covered Himalayas in the background, while the foreground of the picture represented what appeared to be a Chinese pagoda, with a small lake and wooded hills at a distance.

"These pictures," the Master explained, "represent the various monasteries or lamaseries of our order. The one before you is situated near a lake in the interior of Tibet and occupied by some of the highest Adepts of our order. Each of these pictures also shows a part of the country where the monastery is located to give a correct idea of the general character of the locality. But these pictures have an occult quality which will become apparent to you if you concentrate your mind upon some part of the picture."

I did as directed and concentrated on the grand portal of the lamasery. To my astonishment, the door opened, and a tall Indian man, dressed in shining white robes with a turban of pale-yellow silk, stepped out of the door. I immediately recognized him as one of the Tibetan Adepts I had seen in my waking dreams. He, too, seemed to recognize me and smilingly nodded while I bowed reverentially before him. A fine-looking horse was brought by some attendant, which he mounted and rode away.

I was speechless, but the Imperator smiled and drew me away, quoting a passage of Shakespeare with a little modification, for he said, "There are many things in Heaven and Earth which your philosophers don't understand."

We passed on to another picture of Egyptian scenery, with a convent in the foreground and pyramids at a distance; it was gloomier than the former, probably because of the surrounding desert. The next picture represented a similar building in a tropical and mountainous country, and the Adept told me it was somewhere in the Cordilleras of South America. Another one showed a Mohammedan temple, with minarets and the half-moon upon their tops. I was surprised to see all the various religious systems in the world represented in these Rosicrucian orders, for I had always believed that the Rosicrucians were an eminently Christian order.

The Imperator, again reading my thought, corrected my mistake. "The name *Rosicrucian Order*, or the *Order of the Golden and Rosy Cross*," he said, "is a comparatively modern invention and was first used by Johann Valentin Andreae, who invented the story of the knight Christian Rosencreuz for the same purpose as Cervantes invented his *Don Quijote de la Mancha*, namely, to ridicule the would-be Adepts, reformers, and gold-makers of his age when he wrote his celebrated *Fama Fraternitatis*. Before his pamphlet appeared, the name Rosicrucian didn't mean a person belonging to a certain organized society of that name; it was a generic name given to all Occultists, Adepts, Alchemists, or anybody who was or pretended to have some occult knowledge and acquainted with the secret signification of the *Rose* and the *Cross*; symbols which have been adopted by the Christian Church, which were, however, not invented by it, but used by all occultists thousands of years before Christianity was known. These symbols don't belong exclusively to the Christian Church, nor can they be monopolized by it. They are as free as the air for anyone who can grasp their meaning. Unfortunately, very few Christians know that meaning; they only worship the external forms and know nothing about the living principle which those forms represent."

"Then," I said, "someone who is spiritually enlightened may become a member of your order, even if they don't believe in any of the so-called *Christian* dogmas?"

To this, the Imperator answered: "No one can become a member of our exalted order whose knowledge is merely based upon dogmas, beliefs, creeds, or opinions which have been taught to them by somebody, or which they have accepted from hearsay or from the reading of books. Such imaginary knowledge is not *real*; we can know nothing real except what we realize within ourselves because we *feel*, *see*, and *understand* it. That which is usually called *knowledge* is merely a matter of memory. We may store innumerable things in our memory, and they may be true or false; but even if they are true, they don't convey real knowledge. Real knowledge cannot be imparted by one person to another; someone can only be guided to the place where they may obtain it; but they must grasp the truth for themselves, not merely intellectually with their brain but also intuitively with their heart.

"To obtain real knowledge, we must feel the truth of a thing, understand that it is true, and know why it cannot be otherwise. To believe in the truth of anything without having real knowledge of its truth is merely a superstition. And therefore, all your scientific, philosophical, and theological speculations are based upon superstition and not real knowledge. The science and knowledge of your modern philosophers and theologians are continually in danger of being overthrown by some new discovery which won't amalgamate with their artificial systems because the latter are built upon sensual perceptions and logical argumentation. The truth cannot be overthrown; it needs no argumentation, and if it is once perceived by the *spiritual* power of perception and understood by the *spiritual* intelligence of human beings, it conveys real knowledge to the latter and cannot be disputed away.

"Our order has, therefore, nothing to do with creeds or beliefs or opinions of any kind. We care nothing for them; we only want real knowledge. If we were all sufficiently perfect to recognize all truths by direct perception, we should not need any books or instruments; we should not need to use logic or do any experiments. But if we were in such a state of perfection, we should not be here; we should be in *Nirvana*. As it is, we are still beings, although far above the intellectual animal, usually called *human* and

hasn't been *regenerated*. We still use our books and have a library
to study thinkers' opinions. Still, we never accept such books or
opinions — even if they came from Buddha — as our infallible
guides unless they receive the seal from our reason and understanding. We venerate them and use them; they serve us, but we don't
serve them."

During this conversation, we walked into the library, where
thousands of books were standing on many shelves. I noticed many
ancient books which I had heard of but never seen. There were the
Sibylline Books, which are said to have been destroyed by fire; the
books of Hermes Trismegistus, of which only one is believed to
exist; and many others of priceless value for the antiquary or the
student of hermetic philosophy. While I wondered how the Brothers came into possession of such treasures, the Imperator said:

"Well may you be surprised how we came into possession of
books which are no longer supposed to exist; but the secret of
this is that everything, and consequently every book which ever
existed, leaves its imperishable impression in the *Astral Light* and
that by certain occult means these impressions may be reproduced
from that universal storehouse, the memory of Nature, and be put
in a visible, tangible, and material shape. Some of our Brothers are
to a great extent engaged in making such reproductions, and thus
we have without any financial expenses obtained these treasures,
which no amount of money could have procured."

I rejoiced to hear these words because they confirmed my
opinion that life in solitude wasn't necessarily a life of uselessness
and that ideas are real things, which may be seen and grasped far
more easily in a tranquil place than surrounded by the turmoil and
petty cares of life in "society."

In answer to this thought, the Imperator said: "Our monastery was founded by spiritually enlightened people who had the
same thought which I read in your mind. They, therefore, selected
this spot in a secluded valley, whose existence is known only to a
few, and by making use of certain elementary forces of Nature,
which are as yet unknown to you, they created an illusion which

renders this place safe against all unwelcome intruders. Here those in whom the germ of divinity, being latent or dormant in the heart of everyone, has awakened and activity may find the conditions required for its further development. Here we live in peace, separated from the outer world by an impassable barrier, for even if its existence was known, it would be an easy matter to create other illusions to prevent intrusion. We are, however, not excluded from that outer world, although we never enter it with our physical forms. By exercising our clairvoyant and clairaudient powers, we may at any moment know what is going on. And, if we desire to come into personal contact with it, we leave our physical forms and go out in our *astral bodies*. We visit whomsoever we wish and witness everything without our presence being perceived. We visit the statesperson, the minister, the philosopher, and the inventor; we infuse thoughts in their minds which are useful, and they don't know from whence those thoughts come. If their prejudices and predilections are very strong, they may reject those thoughts. But, if they are reasonable and know how to discriminate, they will follow the silent advice and profit by it."

"In that case," I said, "your order can exercise a tremendous influence in the world's politics, so why didn't you try to abolish some of the greatest evils that have afflicted the world? Why did you permit such monsters as Nero and Caligula to exist? Why did you permit the horrors of the Inquisition? Why did you allow the terrors of the French Revolution? Why didn't you destroy such villains as Louis XI of France and others of that class?"

To this, the Adept answered: "There is a certain Law of Justice, which we need to observe, because its action is expedient for the evolution of the race, although people may perceive as evil those consequences which they caused. As the surgeon sometimes has to inflict pain to remove a cancerous growth and save the patient's life, it is often necessary to purge the organism of a nation to restore its health. It is said that evils are blessings in disguise, and God may execute His purpose through the instruments available at His disposal."

"Nevertheless," I said, "it seems to me that you might interfere in individual cases to protect people from committing acts of imprudence which will cause them to suffer."

To this, he replied: "It is true that, by setting a great amount of will-power into motion, we might handle humankind as if they were mere automata, and we could cause them to do what we please, while they would still imagine that they were following their own inclination. But to do so would be against the rules of our order and against the great Law, for the latter decides that each person shall be the creator of their own *Karma*. We are permitted to advise people, but we are not permitted to interfere with their freedom."

"Still," I persisted, "there are innocent people who have to suffer for others' actions; there were martyrs who underwent torture and death for the sake of some great cause. Why didn't you save them? Why did you permit Hypatia to be torn to pieces by a fanatical mob or Joan of Arc to die an ignominious death upon the stake?"

"Such people will have their reward. From the blood of a martyr springs fruit in abundance. Their bodily sufferings are nothing in comparison with the joy they earn. Nothing is useless, although you narrow-sighted mortals cannot always see the use of a thing. Moreover, it often happens that worthy people are saved in a manner appearing to you miraculous."

A strong desire to become a member of the Rosicrucian Society entered my mind, but I didn't dare to express it. The Master, however, reading my mind, continued to say:

"We accept in our circle everyone who has the necessary qualifications to enter it, no matter to what religious belief they may have adhered before obtaining true knowledge; but you will perceive that these qualifications are not in everybody's possession; they cannot be conferred by favour, and it is a well-known saying, even among the lowest grades of occultists, that the Adept cannot be made, but that must grow to become one."

"Master," I said, "would it not be well for those who desire to develop spiritually and to become Adepts to imitate your example and to select some secluded place where they could reside undisturbed and give their time to meditation and concentration of thought? There are a great many people in various parts of the world, belonging to various nationalities and creeds, who have become convinced that the conditions under which the majority of our present civilization live are not conducive to the quick attainment of a higher spiritual state. They believe the objects which they usually strive to attain during their comparatively short lives upon this globe — such as the gratification of pride and ambition, the hoarding of money, the enjoyment of sexual 'love,' the obtaining of bodily comfort and pleasure, etc. — cannot be the true objects of life; but that our present life is only one of the many phases of our eternal existence, and that terrestrial life is only a means to an end, namely, to afford the conditions by which the divine element, germinally contained in everyone, may grow and develop, whereby we may attain a higher life like yours, which isn't subject to transformation and death, and is therefore of permanent value."

The Adept, who had patiently listened to my outburst, smiled and said: "If those people have advanced so far as to be able to bear a life of seclusion, let them enter it; but to do so, it is above all necessary that they possess some real knowledge. Only those who possess such knowledge will be able to live harmoniously together. As long as humanity moves merely on the plane of beliefs and opinion, each person's opinions and tastes will differ from those of the others to a certain extent, and I am afraid that your proposed harmonious society would prove in the end to be a very inharmonious one, and not at all conducive to that tranquillity necessary for interior concentration.

"I have, however, no doubt that even under such unfavourable auspices, that considerable advantage might be derived from the establishment of *theosophical monasteries* in secluded places. If you had any colleges, seminaries, schools, or societies where the truth could be taught without all the accompanying rubbish of scientific and theological misconceptions and superstitions, which have accumulated through the ages, great progress would undoubtedly be made. As the present civilization now stands, there are two education methods. One utilizes what is called *Science*, the other what is called *Religion*. As far as science is concerned, the deductions and speculations are based on observation and logic. The logic may be good enough; but the powers of observation, upon which the fundamentals of its logic rest, are restricted to the very imperfect faculties of sensual perception, and therefore your science is based entirely upon external illusions and is consequently a superficial and illusive science, knowing nothing about the inner life, which is far more important than external phenomena. Scientific doctrines regarding the fundamental laws of Nature are wrong, and therefore all the deductions are wrong as soon as it leaves the plane of illusions.

"You must not misunderstand me," he continued, seeing that I didn't fully grasp the meaning of his words. "I don't mean to say that your modern science knows nothing about the external appearances of things. It knows what it sees and understands, but not being able to see anything except external and sensual phenomena, science only knows external effects. It knows little or nothing about the invisible causes which produce such visible effects, and as soon as it attempts to speculate about them, it errs; because causes are not the consequences of their effects but the consequences of still more interior and fundamental causes, of which modern science knows absolutely nothing, and which, therefore, cannot serve as a basis from which to draw logical conclusions concerning their ultimate effects. Science knows a great deal about the little details of existence which are the ultimate effects of the action of universal Life; but knows nothing about the Tree of Life, the eternal source from which all these transient phenomena spring.

"As far as your modern theology is concerned, it is based upon an entire misconception of terms originally intended to signify certain spiritual powers, of which your priests and laypeople can have no correct conception because they haven't the spiritual powers necessary to conceive of such things. They dispute with each other about the qualities of certain principles, while neither the one nor the other party knows anything whatever about the object of their disputation. Being narrow-minded, the universal principles and powers which are active within the great workshop of Nature have, in their conceptions, become narrowed down to personal and limited beings; the divine and infinite power which humans call *God*, which exists everywhere and without which nothing can possibly exist, has been reduced in the minds of the ignorant to an extra-cosmic deity of some kind, who can be persuaded by mortals to change His will, and who needs substitutes and deputies upon this Earth to execute His Divine Laws. Your religion isn't the religion of the living God who still lives and executes His own will; it is the religion of a dead, impotent god who died long ago and left an army of clergy to rule in His stead. Therefore, your modern religions are systems of superstitions from which the truth has been excluded; the infinite God has been deposed from His eternal throne in the hearts of men and women, and fallible mortal priests have been put in His place. Love has departed, and fear rules humanity; each individual seeks his or her happiness and forgets the existence of others. Each one wants to be saved at the expense of another; each one wants to obtain a reward they haven't merited; all think that to live is the object of life, and few realize the fact that life can have only one reasonable object, namely, to benefit humanity, and can only hope to live eternally by obtaining the power to live, not in their perishable self, but in the spiritual element of humanity.

"Your theology should above all be based upon the power spiritually to perceive the truth. But where can you find a minister who has any spiritual perceptions and dares to trust their intuition more than the dogmas prescribed by their Church? If they dared to have their own opinion and assert it, they would cease to be a minister of the Church and be considered a heretic. In your 'intellectual' age, everything is left to intellectual investigation alone; little is done to develop the intuitive power of the heart. The consequence is that your present generation is like people looking at everything through a telescope; they may see, but they don't *feel* what they see to grasp the truth. The consequence is an entirely false conception of Nature and humankind.

"Humans are neither more nor less than a living organism or instrument through which the *Universal One Life* acts. In so far, they are merely intellectual animals. But the human organization, especially the brain, is far superior to that of animals and therefore enabled to become an instrument for manifesting the highest principle in the Universe, the Principle of Divine Wisdom.

"The instrument, or organism, through which the divine principle acts in and through humans, from within outward, upon the external world, is the organism of the Soul. In this organism, the universal and undifferentiated Divine Spirit finds the soil to grow in an individualized form; it finds the stimulus for its development and the food from which it may draw its strength."

III

UNEXPECTED REVELATIONS

The Adept paused, and multiple questions invaded my mind to which I couldn't find an answer: "What is Nature, and what is human? Why am I in this world? Did I exist before? And, if so, where did I come from? What is the object of my existence, and how will it end?"

Again the Adept, reading my thoughts, answered: "Mortal human beings, as you know them, are intellectual animals, living a sort of dream life among dream pictures which they mistake for realities. Real humans are celestial beings, souls dwelling temporarily within material bodies. Within this organism, the spiritual, divine spark finds the proper soil to generate and develop the immortal human, as has been described by Saint Paul, who speaks of that spark of divine consciousness as sown in corruption and raised in incorruption. This spiritual human is in each person, their personal God and Redeemer. While people are unacquainted with the processes in their invisible organism, they will have little power to guide and control these processes. They will resemble a plant; its existence depends on the elements which are unconsciously brought to it by the winds and the rains or which may accidentally be found in its surroundings; it has neither the power to prevent nor to promote its growth. But when someone obtains knowledge of the constitution of their soul, when they become conscious of the processes in their organism and learn to guide and control them, they will be able to command their growth. They will become free to select or reject the psychic influences within their sphere. They will become their own master and attain — so to say — psychic locomotion. They will then be as much superior to others without such knowledge and power as an animal is superior to a plant; for a while, an animal may go in search of its food and select or reject what it pleases, and the plant is chained to its place and depends entirely on the conditions which that one place affords. The ignorant depend on the conditions prepared for them; the wise can choose their own conditions.

"For many centuries, a superstitious belief prevailed — that a human was a finished being, incapable of further organic improvement. It was, of course, known that during their lifetime, their knowledge could grow and that as they age, they could learn things they didn't know when they were young. Still, thought and intellectual activity was looked upon as something incomprehensible, as a force without matter, as an activity without substance, as nothing. They didn't know where humans stored their acquired knowledge or what became of it when they died. They didn't know whether the body would have another life after death or even perhaps a greater opportunity to acquire knowledge. And if they could learn something after 'death' and without having a body, what was the object of having any physical body at all? None could tell."

"And what will be the end and object of this?" I asked.

"The end of it," was the answer, "is that the soul enjoys supreme bliss in realizing that they are everything and that there is nothing beyond them. The object is that mortals shall become immortal, and a perfect instrument for the manifestation of Divine Wisdom."

I heard the Master's answer but couldn't grasp its meaning. What could that "soul" be of which he spoke as being as big as the Universe, and could mine possess any other vehicle or organism than my visible material body?

While I was meditating, the Adept took me to a window and, pointing out the inaccessible mountain, said: "Behold there the door by which you entered our stronghold. Concentrate your attention on the way you came. Seek with the eye of your soul to penetrate to the other side of the mountain."

I did so, and suddenly I found myself standing on the other side of the mountain, where I had lain down to rest. Before me, stretching out upon the ground, was a lifeless body. To my horror, I recognized it as mine. At first, everything seemed like a dream, but then the thought came to me that I must have died.

There was my body, and nevertheless, I was myself. I saw myself as I had always been, with all my organs and limbs and even the same clothing. I attempted to lift the corpse's hat to reveal its eyes, but I might just as well have tried to lift the inaccessible mountain. There was no physical strength in my arms. I realized that my present body consisted of a state of matter differing from that of the physical plane.

I thought I must have died, and a feeling of disgust overcame me. Thinking I had ever inhabited that now lifeless, grossly material form. I was so glad to be free and had no wish to re-enter it.

But an inner voice seemed to speak to me, saying that the time of my labouring in the mundane sphere hadn't yet ended, and I must return. I even felt a sort of pity for that helpless body, and the sympathy caused thereby created a strong attraction. I felt drawn towards it and was about to lose consciousness when the Master's voice called me away. I started as one who awakes from a dream; the Adept stood by my side, and the vision was gone.

"Know now, my friend," he said, "the difference between your physical and your psychical or astral organism. The divine soul has many vehicles through which it may act and manifest its powers."

"But why," I asked, "are these things not recognized by academical science?"

"On account of self-conceit," answered the Adept. "The scientists, up to recently, used to discard such questions as unworthy. They preferred annihilation over confessing that there was something in the wide expanse of Nature they didn't already know. The theories advanced by the theologians were not more satisfactory than those of the scientists, for they believed — or professed to believe — that humans were complete beings, having come in a finished state out of the hands of their Creator and, as a punishment for their subsequent bad behaviour, having been imprisoned upon this planet. Furthermore, they believed that if someone leading a pious life or, after leading a wicked life, obtained pardon for their sins and the favour of God, they would, after death, become a celestial being, be ushered into a paradise, and live there forever in a state of never-ending enjoyment.

"It will be acknowledged by every independent thinker that these theories were not very satisfactory to those who desired to know the truth. But there was nothing to prove or contradict such assumptions, and, moreover, the multitude didn't think; they paid the clergy to do their thinking for them.

"Since the publication of *Esoteric Buddhism* by A. P. Sinnett, the opinions of the scientists and those of the theologians have been equally shaken to their foundations. The old truth which was known to the ancients, but which had been almost entirely forgotten during our modern age of materialism, that a human isn't a finished being, incapable of any further organic development, but that the body and mind are continually subject to transformation and change, and that no transformation can take place where no substance exists, because force cannot exist without substance, has become almost universally known. It was demonstrated to the scientists that their science extended only to a very small portion of that mysterious being called *humans*. They only knew their outward appearance, their shell, but nothing of the living power acting within that mask called *the physical body*. It was demonstrated to the presumptuous theologians who believed that a person's eternal welfare or damnation depended on their blessings or curses, that justice can't be separated from God, and that God alone is immortal. It was made logically comprehensible to the intellect that God is the divine spiritual element in everyone that walks on Earth, which alone will continue to live after all the lower and imperfect elements are dissolved, and that, therefore, someone in whom God didn't exist in a state of divinity couldn't, after the death of their body, jump into a higher state for which they were unfit and unable to attain while alive.

"The exposition of the essential constitution of a human being, known to the Indian sages, described three hundred years ago by Theophrastus Paracelsus, and again set forth more fully and clearly than ever before by A. P. Sinnett, is calculated to humble the pride of scientists and the vanity of priests. When it is once more known and digested, it will prove to the learned how little they know, and it will draw a line for the legitimate activity of the clergy as an instructor in morals. It proves that men and women are not already gods as some had imagined themselves to be. It proves that someone may look like an intellectual giant and still be, spiritually considered, only diminutive. It demonstrates that the law governing organisms' growth on the physical plane isn't reversed when it acts within the corresponding organisms on the psychical plane. It shows that out of nothing, nothing can grow, but wherever there is the germ of something, even if that germ is invisible, something may grow and develop.

"The growth of every germ and of every being, as far as we know it, depends on certain conditions. These conditions may be established either using intellectual activity, which the being has the power to surround itself with or by external causes over which the being has no control. A plant or animal cannot grow unless it receives the necessary food and the stimulus. The intellect cannot expand unless it is fed with ideas and stimulated by reason to assimilate them. The spirit cannot become strong unless it finds in the lower principles the nutriment required to acquire strength and is stimulated by the light of wisdom to select what it requires."

Here again, the thought occurred to me how agreeable and profitable it would be to live in a Rosicrucian convent, where everything was rendered comfortable, no disturbing elements being admitted.

To this, the Master answered: "One element necessary for the development of strength is resistance. If we enter one of the vast pine forests of the Alps or the Rocky Mountains in the United States, we find ourselves surrounded by towering trees whose main trunks have very few branches. Upwards they rise like the masts of a ship, covered with grey bark, naked, and without foliage. Only near the tops that reach out of the shadows do they throw upon each other. The branches appear and spread to the highest points, which wave their heads in the sunlight. These trees are all top-heavy; their chiefly or only well-developed parts are their heads, and all the life which they extract from the ground and the air seems to mount to their tops; while the trunks, although increasing in size as the tree grows, are left undeveloped and bare of branches. Thus they may stand and grow from year to year and reach a mature age. But someday, sooner or later, some dark clouds collect around the snowy peaks and assume a threatening aspect. The gleam of lightning appears among the swelling masses, thunder is heard, bolts of liquid light dart from the rents in the clouds, and suddenly the storm sweeps down from the summit into the valley. Then the work of devastation begins. These top-heavy trees, having but little strength in their feet, are mowed down by the wind like so many stems of straw in a wheat field; there they lie rank after rank, having tumbled over each other in their fall, and their corpses encumber the mountainsides. But at the edge of the timber and outside of the main body of the forest, looking like outposts or sentinels near the lines of a battle, there are still here and there some solitary pines undamaged by the storm. They have, on account of their isolated positions, been exposed to winds all their lives; they have become used to it and grown strong. They haven't been protected and sheltered by their neighbours. They are not top-heavy, for their great strong branches grow out from the trunk a few feet above the soil, continuing up to the tops, and their roots have grown through the crevices of the rocks, holding on to them with an iron grasp. They have met with resistance since their youth and, by resisting, have gained their strength.

"Thus, an intellectual, growing up protected by fashion and friends in a school, college, university, or perhaps within the walls of a convent or monastery, finds themselves isolated from contrary influences and meets only a little resistance. Crowded together with those who think similarly, they live and think like the others. Over their heads waves the banner of some accepted authority, and upon it are inscribed certain dogmas in which they believe without ever daring to doubt their veracity. There they grow, throwing upon each other the shadow of their ignorance, preventing each other from seeing the sunlight of truth. There they cram their brains with authorized opinions, learning many of the details of our illusory life, which they mistake for real existence. They become top-heavy, for all the energy they receive from the universal fountain of life goes to supply the brain; the heart is left without a supply. The strength of character, of which the heart is the seat, suffers. The intellect is overfed, and the spirit is starved. Thus they may grow up and become proud of their knowledge, but perhaps someday, new and strange ideas appear on the mental horizon, a wind begins to blow and down tumbles the banner upon which their dogmas have been inscribed, and their pride tumbles down with it.

"But not only on the physical and the intellectual plane; in the realm of the emotions, too, the same law prevails. Those who desire to develop strength mustn't be afraid of resistance; they must obtain strength in their feet. They must be prepared to meet the wind of contrary opinions and not be overthrown when the storms of passion arise. They should force themselves to remain in contact with that which is not according to their taste and even to harmonize with that which appears inimical, for it is really their friend because it can supply them with strength. They should learn to bear calumny and animosity, envy and opposition, endure suffering and estimate life at its true value. The contrary influences they have been exposed to may cause a tempest to rage through their hearts, but when they have gained the power to command the tempest to cease and to say to the excited waves of their emotions: 'Be still!' — then the first gleam of the rising sun will appear in their hearts, and before its warm glow, the cold moonlight thrown out by the calculating and reflecting brain will grow pale; a new and still larger world than the external one will appear before their interior vision, where they'll be contented to live and find an inexhaustible source of happiness, unknown to those who live a life of the senses. Henceforth they will require no more to speculate reflectively about the truth, for they will see it clearly in their hearts. Henceforth they won't be required to be exposed to storms but may seek shelter in a tranquil place; not because they are afraid of the storms, which can do them no harm, but because they want to employ their energies for the full development of the newly awakened spiritual germ, instead of wasting them uselessly on the outward plane.

"What the disciple ought to seek is to strengthen their character, which constitutes real individuality, keeping it always in harmony with the Law of Divine Wisdom and Love. Someone without the strength of character is without true individuality, without self-reliance, moved only by the emotions which arise in their mind and belong to powers foreign to their divine nature.

"Only after the attainment of a certain state of maturity, life in solitude, isolated from contrary influences, becomes desirable and useful, and those who retire from the world as long as they need the world are attempting to ascend to the Kingdom of Heaven by beginning at the top of the ladder. Let the person who needs the world remain in the world. The greater the temptations, the greater their strength if they successfully resist. Only those who can within their own mental sphere create the conditions their spirit requires are independent of all external conditions and free. Those who can't evolve a world within their soul need the external world to evolve it.

"*Unspiritual* people, therefore, who retire from the world because they are afraid of the world, can't be considered heroes and heroines who have renounced the world; they deserve rather to be regarded as cowards who have deserted their ranks at the beginning of the battle with life. Such people sometimes retire to convents to have a comfortable life, in addition to a ticket to Heaven. They imagine they do a service to God by leading a harmless, useless life, for which imaginary service they expect to obtain a reward at its end. But the reward will also exist merely in their imagination. As the sensualist wastes their time in the prosecution of useless pleasures, so the bigot wastes their time in useless ceremonies. The actions of the former are instigated by a desire for sensual pleasure in this life, those of the latter by the hope for pleasure in another life — both act to gratify their own selfish desires. I cannot see any essential difference between the motives and morals of the two.

"But with a *spiritually developed* person, the case is entirely different. The divine principle exists independent of the conditions of relative space and time; it is eternal and self-existent. It cannot be angered by the opposition, irritated by contradiction, nor thrown into confusion by sophistry. If it has once become conscious of its own power, it won't require the stimulus needed by the physical organism and afforded by the impressions which come through the avenues of the senses from the outer world, for it is itself that stimulus which creates worlds within its own substance. It is the Lord over all the elemental animal forces in one's soul, and their turmoil can neither educate nor degrade it, for it is Divinity in a pure state — eternal, unchangeable, and free."

"Do you mean to say," I asked, "that all asceticism and self-denial are useless?"

And the Master answered: "It all depends upon the motive. All the egotist does for their own selfish progress and aggrandizement is useless; it is done for an illusion and increases self-conceit. But this you will understand only when the consciousness of the divine state awakens within you, and you begin to realize the difference between your true and your illusive self.

"The one in whom this divine principle has once awakened, who has once practically experienced the inner life, who has visited the Kingdom of Heaven within their soul, who stands firm upon their feet, will no more need the educating influences of the contending storms of the outer world, to gain strength by resistance; nor will they experience any desire to return to the pleasures and tomfooleries of the world. They renounced nothing when they retired into the solitude, for it cannot be looked upon as an act of renunciation if we throw away a thing which is a burden to us. This person cannot be called an *ascetic*, for they don't undergo any discipline or process of hardening; it is no act of self-denial to refuse things we don't want. The true ascetic is the man or woman who lives in the world, surrounded by its temptations; in whose soul the animal elements are still active, craving for the gratification of their desires and possessing the means for their gratification, but who by the superior power of their will conquers their animal self. Having attained that state, they may retire from the world and employ their energies for employment and the further expansion of their spiritual power. They will be perfectly happy because they can create their desires in their own interior world. They expect no future reward of happiness in Heaven as they already possess it. They desire no other good but to create good for the world.

"If you could establish theosophical monasteries where intellectual and spiritual development went hand in hand, where a new science could be taught, based upon true knowledge of the fundamental laws of the Universe, and where at the same time people would be taught how to obtain mastery over themselves, you would confer the greatest possible benefit upon the world. Such a convent would, moreover, afford immense advantages for the advancement of intellectual research. The establishment of several such places of learning would dot the mental horizon of the world with stars of the first magnitude, from which rays of intellectual light would stream and penetrate. Standing upon a far higher plane than the material science of our times, a new and far greater field would be laid open for investigation and research in these centres. Knowing all the different opinions of the highest accepted authorities, and not being bound by an orthodox scientific creed, having at their service all the results of the investigations of the learned, but not being bound to their systems by a belief in their infallibility, such people would be at liberty to think freely. Their convents would become centres of intelligence, illuminating the world. And if their power of self-control would grow in equal proportion with the development of their intellect, they would soon be able to enter Adeptship."

The Adept had spoken these words with unusual warmth as if intending to appeal to my sympathy and induce me to establish such places. There was a look of pity in his eyes as if he exceedingly regretted the state of poor ignorant humanity, with whose Karma he wasn't permitted to interfere forcibly, according to the established rules of his order. I, too, regretted my own inability, and for once, I wished that I were rich to make at least an attempt with one such establishment. But immediately, the Imperator saw my thought in my mind and said:

"You mistake; it is not the want of money which prevents us from executing this idea; it is the impossibility of finding the proper kind of people to inhabit the convent after it is established. Indeed, we would be poor alchemists if we couldn't produce gold in any desirable quantity if some real benefit for humanity could be affected. I shall convince you of this if you desire it. But gold is a curse to humankind, and we don't wish to increase people's suffering. Distribute gold, and you will only create a craving for more; give them power, and you will transform them into devils. No, it is not gold we need; it is people who thirst after true wisdom. Thousands desire knowledge, but few desire wisdom. Intellectual development, sagacity, craftiness, and cunning are today mistaken for spiritual development, but this conception is wrong. Animal cunning isn't intelligence, craftiness isn't wisdom, and most of your learned people are the last ones who can bear the truth. Even many of your would-be occultists and so-called Rosicrucians have taken up their investigations merely to gratify their idle curiosity. In contrast, others desire to pry into the secrets of Nature to obtain knowledge that they hope to employ to attain selfish ends. Give us men or women who desire nothing else but the truth, and we will take care of their needs. How much money will it require to lodge a person who cares nothing for comfort? What will it take to furnish the kitchen for those who have no desire for dainties? What libraries will be required for those who can read the book of Nature? What external pictures will please those who wish to avoid a life of the senses and retire within themselves? What terrestrial scenery shall be selected for those who live within the paradise of their souls? What company will please those who converse with their own higher self? How can we amuse those who live in the presence of God?"

Here the Adept paused for a moment and then continued, saying: "The theosophical monastery of which I dream is even superior to ours. It is far from this Earth, yet it can be reached without trouble and expense. Its monks and nuns have risen above the sphere of self. They have a temple of infinite dimensions, pervaded by the spirit of sanctity, which is the common possession of all. There the differentiation of the Universal Soul ceases, and Unification takes place. It is a convent where no difference of gender, taste, opinion, and desire exists; where vice cannot enter; where none are born, or marry, or die, but where they live like the angels; each one constituting the centre of a power for good; each one immersed in an infinite ocean of light; each one able to see all they desire to see, to know all they want to know, growing in strength and expanding in size, until embracing the All and is one with it."

For a moment, it seemed as if the soul of the Adept had gone and visited that blissful state of Nirvana, a state of which we mortals cannot conceive. Still, soon the light returned into his eyes, and he smilingly excused himself, saying that he had permitted himself to be carried away by the sublimity of this idea. I ventured to say that probably millions of ages would pass away before humankind arrived at that state.

"Alas!" he answered, "the conditions which our present state of civilization imposes upon its followers are now such as to force the vast majority of humanity to employ nearly all their time and energy in an outward direction instead of employing them for their inward growth. Each person has a certain amount of energy they may call their own. If they waste all that energy on the outward plane, either for the attainment of sensual gratification or intellectual pursuits, they will have nothing left to nourish the divine germ in their heart. If someone continually concentrates their mind outwardly, there will be no inward concentration of thought, which is absolutely necessary to attain self-knowledge. The labouring classes, those of commerce, scientists, doctors, lawyers, and clergy, are all actively engaged in outward affairs and find little time for the inward concentration of their powers. The majority are continually occupied running after shadows and illusions, which are at best only useful as long as they last but whose usefulness ceases when the heart ceases to beat. Their time and energy are taken up in procuring what they call the *necessities of life*, and they excuse themselves by saying that it is their misfortune to be so situated as to be forced to procure them. Nature, however, cares nothing for our excuses; the law of cause and effect is blind and inaccessible to argumentation. Someone climbing over a mountaintop and falling over a precipice is as much in danger of breaking their neck as if they had jumped down voluntarily; a man or woman unable to progress will be left as far behind as one who doesn't desire to progress. But Nature isn't so cruel as she appears to be to the superficial observer. That which humans require for the purpose of living is very little indeed and can usually be easily obtained; for Nature has amply provided for all of her children, and if they cannot all obtain their proper share, then there must be something seriously wrong, either with them individually or with the social organization as a whole. There is undoubtedly a great deal wrong in our social organization, and our philosophers and politicians are continually trying to remedy it. They will succeed in their task when they make the laws of the human world harmonize with the laws of Nature, and not before. That event may take place in the far distant future. We don't have the time to wait for it. Let each attempt to restore harmony in their own individual organism and live according to natural laws, and the harmony of the social organism as a whole will be restored."

The words of the Adept caused me some confusion, for I loved the comforts of life. A spirit of contradiction arose and caused me to ask: "Would you, then, do away with all luxuries, which at our present stage of civilization have become necessities? I know certain cranks harbour such views."

"Not so," answered the Adept. "The great bulk of those things which are said to be the necessities of life are only artificially created necessities, and millions of people lived and attained old age long before many of the things our modern civilization considers as absolutely necessary had been discovered or invented. The term *necessity* has a relative meaning. To a monarch, a dozen palaces, to a noble, a carriage and four may appear as a necessity as a bottle of whisky to a beggar or a swallowtail coat to a fashionista. To get rid at once of all such fancied necessities and the trouble which is imposed upon us to attain them, the shortest and surest way is to rise above such necessities and to consider them not to be necessary at all. Then a great amount of our energy would become free and might be employed to acquire what is really necessary because it is eternal and permanent. At the same time, that which serves merely temporal purposes ends in time.

"There are thousands of people engaged in prying into the details of the constitution of external objects and in learning the chemical and physiological processes going on therein, and some are sacrificing their soul and extinguishing the spark of divinity within themselves by perpetrating the most inhuman cruelties upon their fellow beings to gratify their scientific curiosity and make useless discoveries for the promotion of their ambition. But they don't manifest the least curiosity to know their own constitution and the processes within their own organization. However, it would seem that such a knowledge of the latter is far more important than an investigation of the former. Modern science says that it wants to know the laws of Nature in all their minute ramifications and yet pays no attention whatever to the universal and fundamental law from which all these ramifications spring. Thus science resembles an insect crawling over a fallen leaf and imagining, thereby learning the qualities of the tree. It is surely the prerogative of an intellectual to investigate all the departments of Nature intellectually. But investigating external things is only of secondary importance to attaining knowledge of our own interior powers. All primary powers act from within; effects are secondary to causes. Those who consider the knowledge of external things more important than self-knowledge possess very little wisdom."

"These doctrines," I said, "will never be accepted by our educators; they look upon the very term *Theosophy* with contempt. They believe that a knowledge of external things is the only knowledge attainable, and the only one worth having, and this illusive knowledge they call *exact science*."

"I pity them for their imperfections," answered the Adept; "nevertheless, their views are justifiable from their own standpoint. If they object to the term *Theosophy*, they don't know what it means; as it has often been misapplied, they have formed a misconception about it. We can know nothing except what we know *theosophically*; because theosophical knowledge is the result of feeling, seeing, and understanding a thing. Their sense of seeing and feeling does not penetrate below the external surface of things, and they, therefore, know theosophically merely the outward appearance. The internal causes are left to speculations which are often erroneous. The higher sense, by which the Adept can penetrate with their consciousness into the interior of things and identify with the object of their observation, share its sensations, feel as if they were that object, see the workings of the interior causes, and consequently understand it, is unknown to the scientists of our present civilization."

"And what about God?" I asked. "Is it possible to prove that He exists?"

To this answered the Adept: "I am sorry for anyone who is so backward in their course of spiritual evolution that they can't yet recognize the presence of God in everything. The supreme spirit which pervades, embraces, and penetrates everything, being the essence, soul, and life of all things in the Universe, from the atom to the whole Solar System, is beyond all mental conception. If He could be grasped by the human intellect, that intellect would have to be greater than God. There is nothing real but God. Nature is only a manifestation of His power. Let no one expect that somebody will prove the existence of God but seek to be a living witness of His presence and power by becoming god-like and divine by His Divine Grace. People are destined to restore within themselves the divine image. When they realize the divine ideal within their hearts, their pilgrimage through manifold incarnations will have ended, and the object of existence accomplished. Peace be with you!"

As the Adept finished this sentence, a sound as if produced by the tinkling of small silver bells was heard above our heads. I looked up, but nothing was to be seen from which that sound could have proceeded.

"This is the signal," said the Adept, "that the order is assembled in the refectory. Let us go join them. Some refreshment will undoubtedly be welcome to you."

IV

THE POWER OF IMAGINATION

We stepped out into the corridor and entered the garden. The palm trees and exotic plants surrounding us formed a strong contrast to the weird and desolate scenery, with its fields of ice and scrub pines, which I had seen before entering this enchanted valley. High bushes of fuchsias alternated with rose bushes, and all were covered with the most beautiful flowers. The air was perfumed with the odour of many varieties of hyacinths, heliotropes, and other plants whose names I don't remember. Nevertheless, the place wasn't a hothouse, for there was no other roof over it than the clear blue sky. I wondered whether perhaps the garden was heated from below the surface, and the thought came into my mind that so much luxury didn't seem to agree with the view expressed by the Adept, that those who live within the paradise of their own souls don't care for external sensual gratification. But again, the Imperator seemed to know my thought even before it had taken a definite form in my mind and said:

"We have created these illusions to make your visit agreeable. All these trees and plants require no gardener and are inexpensive; they cost us nothing but an effort of our imagination."

I went up to one of the rose bushes and broke one of the roses. It was a real rose, as real as I had ever seen before; its odour was sweet, and it had just unfolded its leaves in the rays of the midday sun.

"Surely," I said, "this rose which I hold in my hand can't be an illusion or an effect of my imagination?"

"No," answered the Adept, "it isn't produced by your own imagination, but it is a product of the imagination of Nature, whose processes can be guided by the spiritual will of the Adept. The whole world, with its solid planets, its mountains of granite, its oceans and rivers, the whole Earth with all its multifarious forms, is nothing but a product of the imagination of the *Universal Mind*, which is the *creator* of forms. Forms are nothing real. They are merely illusions or shapes of substance; a form without substance is unthinkable and cannot exist. But the only substance we know is the universal primordial element of matter, constituting the substance of the Universal Mind, the *Akasha*. This element of matter is invisibly present everywhere, but only when it assumes a certain state of density, sufficient to resist the penetrating influence of the terrestrial light, does it come within reach of your sensual perception and assume an objective shape. The universal power of will penetrates all things. Guided by the spiritual intelligence of the Adept, whose consciousness pervades all their surroundings, it creates in the Universal Mind those shapes which the Adept imagines; for the sphere of the Universal Mind, where they live, is their own mind, and there is no difference between the latter and the former, as far as the sphere of the latter extends. By an occult process, which can't be at present explained to you, but which exists principally in an effort of will, the shapes thus created in the mind-substance of the Adept are rendered dense and thereby become objective and real to you."

"I acknowledge," I said, "this is still incomprehensible to me. Can an image formed in your head assume a material form?"

The Adept seemed amused at my ignorance and smilingly answered: "Do you believe that the sphere of mind in which someone lives exists only within the circumference of their skull? I should be sorry for such a person, for they wouldn't be able to see or experience anything beyond the processes in that part of their mind contained within the skull. The whole world would be nothing but impenetrable and incomprehensible darkness. They wouldn't be able to see the sun or any external object. For a person can perceive nothing except that which exists within their own mind. Fortunately, the sphere of the mind of each individual reaches as far as the stars. It reaches as far as their power of perception. The mind comes in contact with all things, however distant they may be from the physical body. Thus the mind — not the brain — receives the impressions, and these impressions come to a person's consciousness within their physical brain, which is merely the centre in which the messages of the mind are received."

After giving this explanation, the Adept, evidently still seeing some doubts in my mind, directed me to look at a magnolia tree which stood at a short distance. It was a tree of perhaps sixty feet and covered with great, white, beautiful flowers. While I looked, the tree began to appear less and less dense. The green foliage faded into grey so that the white blossoms could hardly be distinguished from the leaves. It became more shadowy and transparent until it seemed merely the ghost of a tree. Finally, it disappeared entirely from view.

"Thus," continued the Adept, "you see that tree stood in the sphere of my mind as it stood in yours. We are all living within the sphere of each other's minds, and those in whom the power of spiritual perception has been developed may at all times see the images created in the mind of another. The Adept creates their own images; the ordinary mortal lives in the products of the imagination of others, either in those of the imagination of Nature or in those created by other minds. We live in the paradise of our own soul, and the objects which you behold exist in the realm of our soul, but the spheres of our souls are not narrow. They have expanded far beyond the limits of the visible bodies and will continue to expand until they become one with the Universal Soul and as large as the latter.

"The power of the imagination is yet too little known to humankind. Else they would better beware of what they think. If a person thinks a good or evil thought, that thought calls into existence a corresponding form or power within the sphere of their mind, which may assume density and become living, and continue to live long after the physical body of the person who created it has died. It will accompany their soul after death because the creations are attracted to their creator."

"Does, then," I asked, "every evil thought, or the imagination of something evil, create that evil and cause it to exist as a living entity?"

"Not so," answered the Imperator. "Every thought calls into existence the form or power of which we think, but these things have no life until life is infused into them by the Will. If they don't receive life from the Will, they are like shadows and soon fade away. If this wasn't the case, people could never read of a crime without mentally committing it, thereby creating the most vicious

Elementals. You may imagine evil deeds of all kinds, but unless you desire to perform them, the creations of your imagination obtain no life. But if you desire to perform them if your will is so evil that you would be willing to perform them if you had the external means to do so, then it may perhaps be as bad for you as if you had actually committed them. You create thereby a living, although invisible power of evil. The Will endows imagination's creations with life because *Will* and *Life* are fundamentally identical."

Seeing a doubt arise in my mind, he continued: "If I speak of the Will as life-giving power, I am speaking of the spiritual will-power which resides in the heart. A will-power merely exercised by the brain is like the cold moonlight, which has no power to warm the forms upon which it falls. The life-giving will-power comes from the heart and acts like the rays of the sun, which call life into action in minerals, plants, and animals. It is what people desire with their hearts, not what they merely imagine with their brains, which has real power. Fortunately for humankind, very few have this spiritual will-power which calls the creations of the imagination into objective visible existence. Else the world would be filled with living materialized monsters, which would devour humankind. For there are in our present state of civilization more people who harbour evil desires than such as desire the good. But their will isn't spiritual enough to be powerful; it comes more from the brain than from the heart; it is usually only strong enough to harm the one who created the evil thought and to leave others unaffected. Thus you see how important it is that the masses should not possess spiritual powers until they become virtuous and good. In former times, these mysteries were kept very secret. If you use them, be careful to discern good from evil."

We entered through a Gothic portal into a hall. The light fell through four high windows into the room, which was of an octagonal form. Amid this room stood a round table surrounded by chairs, and the corners formed by the sides of the octagon were provided with furniture of various kinds. Many of the Brothers assembled, some of whom I recognized from seeing their pictures in historical representation. There were also two ladies present — one appearing very tall and dignified, the other of smaller stature and of a more delicate, but not less noble, appearance and exceedingly beautiful. To find *women* in the monastery of the Brothers of the Golden and Rosy Cross was a fact that surprised and staggered me, and my confusion was evidently observed by all present. Still, after I had been introduced to all the persons present — or, to express it more correctly, after they were introduced to me, for they seemed to know me and not need introduction — the tall lady took my hand and led me to the table, while smilingly speaking the following words:

"Why should you be so surprised, my friend, to see Adepts inhabiting female forms in the company of those whose forms appear to be of a male character? What has intelligence to do with the body's gender? Where the physical instincts end, there ends the influence of gender. Take this chair by my side and have some of this delicious fruit."

The table was covered with various excellent fruits, some of which I had never seen before and don't grow in this country. The illustrious company took their seats, and a conversation ensued in which all took part. I only too deeply felt my own inferiority while in this place, but everyone seemed to exert their powers to reassure me and to make me imagine that I was their equal. The Brothers and Sisters hardly tasted the food, but they seemed to be pleased to see me enjoy it, and in fact, my morning walk and the pure air of the mountain had given me a very good appetite. The noble lady beside me soon made my embarrassment vanish, answered my questions regarding the causes of certain occult phenomena, and did a few practical experiments to illustrate her doctrines. The following may serve as an example of the powers she possessed to create illusions.

We spoke of the intrepidity and undaunted courage required to enter the realm of occult research: "For," she said, "the whole elemental world, with all its monstrosities and animal elements, is opposed to our spiritual progress. The animals (Elementals) living in the animal principle of our human constitution live on our life energy and the substance of our animal elements. If the divine spirit awakens within the heart and sends its light into those animal elements, the substance on which these parasites live is destroyed, and they begin to rage like other famished beasts. They fight for their lives and food, and they are, therefore, the greatest impediments and opponents to spiritual progress. They live in the lower regions of the soul and are, under normal conditions, invisible to the external senses, although under certain conditions, they may even become visible and objective. They live in families and reproduce like our terrestrial animals; they fight and eat each other. If someone's selfish desires, such as are of a minor type, are all swallowed up by some great master-passion, it merely shows that a *monster elemental* has grown in their soul and devoured all the minor elementals."

I answered that I couldn't believe that a human was such a living and walking menagerie and said I wished I could see one of these elementals to realize what it was.

"Would you not be afraid," she asked, "if such a vicious thing were to appear before you?"

I began to boast of my bravery and said that I was never afraid of anything I could see with my eyes and reach with my hands; that fear was the outcome of ignorance and that knowledge dispelled all fear.

"You are right," she answered, "but will you be so kind as to hand me that basket with pears."

I stretched forth my hand after the basket with pears, which stood in the centre of the table, and as I was about to grasp it, a horrible rattlesnake rose up between the fruit, rearing its head and making a noise with its rattles as if in great anger. Horror-struck, I withdrew my hand, barely escaping its venomous bite. But while I stared at it, the serpent coiled itself up again among the pears, its glistening scales disappeared in the basket and was gone.

"If you had dared to grasp the snake," said one of the Brothers, who had witnessed the scene, "you would have found it to be merely an illusion."

"The Will," remarked the Imperator, "isn't merely a life-giving power; it is also a destroyer. It causes the atoms of primordial

were to act only in harmony with reason, all intellectual human beings would not only be intellectual but would also be wise. But we know from our daily experience that intellectuality isn't necessarily accompanied by wisdom, that often, those who are most cunning are also most vicious. The most learned are often the most unreasonable.

"The first and most important step to take," continued the Brother, "if someone desires to obtain spiritual power, is to become natural. Only when they have thrown off all their unnatural qualities can they hope to become spiritually strong. If someone was to become spiritual before becoming natural, they would be an unnatural monster. Such monsters have existed and still exist. They are the powers of evil acting through human forms; they are the Adepts of Dark Magic, sorcerers and villains of various grades."

"Then," I said, "I presume that great criminals are, to a certain extent, dark magicians."

"Not necessarily so," answered the Brother. "Most evildoers do evil, not for the love of evil, but to attain some selfish purpose. The villains who are on the road to Dark Magic do evil because they love it, in the same sense as those who are on the road to true Adeptship perform well merely because they love good. But whether someone performs good or evil acts, a constant or frequent repetition of such acts causes them to perform them instinctively. Thus their own nature becomes gradually either identified with good or with evil. The one who merely tortures a fly for the sake of torturing it, and because they are pleased to do so, is farther progressed on the road to villainy and absolute evil with consequent destruction than someone who murders another because they imagine it to be necessary for their own protection."

Here the conversation began to turn about the Magic of Light and the wonderful powers of certain Tibetan Adepts. The Imperator, who had recently visited them, gave a detailed account of his visit. But, strange as it may appear, while all the details of the other part of our conversation remained deeply engraved in my memory, the account given by the Imperator about that visit is entirely effaced from my mind, and I can't remember anything whatever about it. It is as if its recollection had been purposely eradicated from my mind.

After our breakfast, the Imperator recommended me to the care of the two Lady-Adepts and told me that he would soon rejoin us to show me his alchemical laboratory. I then accompanied my two protectors into the beautiful garden.

V

THREE SISTERS REUNITED

e passed through an alley formed by oleander bushes in full bloom and arrived at a small round pavilion standing upon a little eminence, which afforded a beautiful view of the country and the mountaintops in the distance. The pavilion's roof was supported by marble columns surrounded by ivy, which grew around the pillars and nearly covered the roof, hanging down at intervals in the open spaces. We seated ourselves, and after a short pause, my friend, whom I will call Layla, said: "I owe you an explanation about the remarks I made when I saw your astonishment at seeing women among the Brothers of the Golden and Rosy Cross. Your intuition told you correctly. It doesn't very often happen that an individual attains Adeptship while inhabiting a female organism because such an organism isn't as well adapted as a male one to develop energy and strength. It is, therefore, frequently the case that those women who have far advanced on the road to Adeptship must reincarnate in a male organism before they can achieve the final result.

"Nevertheless, exceptions are found. You know that the organism of a man isn't fundamentally different from a woman, and everyone is a combination of male and female elements. In women, usually, the female elements preponderate, and in men, the male ones. Although we meet with women of a masculine character and men of a womanish nature. In a perfect human being, the male and female elements are nearly equally strong, with a slight preponderance of the male element, representing the productive power in Nature. In contrast, the female element represents the formative principle. This occult law, which to explain at present would lead us deep into the mysteries of Nature, will become comprehensible to you if you study the laws of harmony and that the greatest beauty finds its expression in the composition of major and minor chords, flats and sharps. Other and numerous analogies may be found, and we shall leave it to your own ingenuity to find them out.

"If you find an Adept inhabiting a female organism, you will be right in concluding that it is due to some extraordinary conditions and experiences through which such an Adept has passed during her last incarnation. A plant in a hot house will grow faster than one which is not cared for, and, likewise, extraordinary suffering may cause the early development of the flower of spirituality, which without such suffering would have taken place, perhaps, much later in some other incarnation."

This revelation stirred my curiosity, and I begged the lady to give me an account of her past life, as it was before she became an Adept.

"It is sometimes painful," answered Layla, "to dwell on past memories, but perhaps our Sister Helen will give you such an account of her life."

The lady addressed smiled and said: "I will certainly do so to afford pleasure to our visitor, but any life in comparison with yours has been very uninteresting. If you proceed with your history, I will add mine at the end."

"Very well, then," answered Layla, "but to simplify matters and save time, I will show you its pictorial representation in the Astral Light. Look upon the table before you."

I looked upon the polished surface of the round marble table standing in the centre of the pavilion, and, as I looked, there appeared upon its surface the life-like image of a battlefield.

The contending armies were fighting with swords and spears, warriors on horseback and some on foot, knights in glistening armour, and common soldiers. Hot grows the fight; the dead and wounded cover the ground, and the soldiers to the left begin to give way while those to the right press forward. Suddenly there appears at the left a beautiful woman, dressed in armour, carrying a sword in one hand and in the other a banner. Her features resemble those of the Lady-Adept. At the sight of her, the men to the left seem to become filled with strength, while their enemies seem to be stricken with terror. The latter flees, pursued by the men on the left, and a shout of triumph arises, and the picture fades away.

Now there appears another picture on the table. It seems to be the interior of a Catholic church. There is a great assembly of dignitaries of church and state, knights and nobles, bishops and priests, and a multitude of people. In front of the altar kneels an armoured knight, who seems to be the king, and a bishop, ornamented with the insignia of his office, puts a golden crown upon his head; but by the side of the king stands a noble-looking woman, with a smile of triumph upon her face and holding a banner. Solemn music is heard, but as the crown rests upon the head of the king and he arises, a thousand voices hail him, and the picture fades away.

The next picture represents a dungeon filled with torture instruments, such as were used at the time of the Inquisition. There are some men dressed in black, and in their eyes burns the fire of hate; there are others dressed in red; they are evidently the executioners. Some people with torches appear, and in their midst is Layla bound with chains. She looks at the men in black with pity and contempt. They ask her some silly questions, which she refuses to answer, and then they begin to torture her cruelly. I averted my sight, and when I looked again, the picture was gone.

In its place appeared another. There is a pile of wood, and in its midst is a stake to which a chain is fastened. A procession approaches, led by villainous-looking monks and guarded by soldiers. Crowds surround the pile, but they give way as the procession approaches. Amid the monks and hangmen walks Layla, looking pale and emaciated from torture and suffering. Her hands are tied, and a rope is fastened around her neck. She mounts the pile and is fastened to the stake. She attempts to speak, but the praying monks dash water into her face to force her to remain silent. A hangman appears with a brand of fire; the wood begins to burn; the flames touch the beautiful woman's body. I desired to see no more. I buried my face in my hands. I knew who Layla was.

After I had recovered from this horrible sight, I expressed my admiration for Layla's valour and virtue. I had always admired her as a historical character and desired to see her portrait. Now she stood before me, the living original, youthful and strong, noble and beautiful, and yet, according to the views of mortals, over four hundred and fifty years of age.

It is useless to attempt to conceal a thought in the presence of the Adepts. Layla observed my thought and answered it.

"No," she said, "I am much older than you think. I and you, and we all, are as old as creation. When the spirit began to breathe after the great *Pralaya* was over, sending out of the centre the light of the *Logos*, which called the world into existence, we lived already, and we shall continue to live until this light returns to its source. Our real *I* knows no age; it remains ever young; it is eternal and independent of the conditions of the time. Nor can our spiritual bodies be destroyed by fire. They are the mirrors in which the spirit reflects its divine image; matter is as eternal as space and spirit, and as long as matter exists, the spirit will reflect its image therein. Spirit requires such an image for the purpose of attaining self-knowledge. A person cannot see their face without the help of a mirror; we can't see ourselves objectively unless we step out of ourselves. Therefore, the spirit reflects its light into matter and sees itself in the mirror."

"But," I said, "your body was destroyed by fire. How is it that I see you before me in a visible, tangible form?"

"That which was destroyed," answered Layla, "was merely the grossest material substance of my physical organization. As the fire consumed the gross matter, my astral form arose above the fire and the smoke. It was invisible to the multitude present, whose senses are so gross that they can only perceive gross matter. But it was visible to the Adepts who were present in their ethereal forms and took care of me, and after a short period of unconsciousness, I awoke again to external life. Gradually my body hardened again by the action of the influences prevailing in my new home. Therefore, I am now as visible and tangible to you as if I were still inhabiting my material form."

"Then, I presume," I said, "that the astral body of every human being or animal could be so hardened after having left the physical form, and thus the spirits of the dead could be made to appear in a tangible and visible form."

"It could be done, and it has often been," answered Layla, "by the vile practices of the necromantic art. It can be done with the Earth-bound astral forms of those who have suddenly died by accident or murder and whose astral forms are still a great deal of molecular adhesion. But the astral forms of those who died a natural death or died long ago cannot be thus evoked because their astral corpses have already been decomposed by the influences of the astral plane. But those 'materialized' forms have no life of their own and cannot endure. They only live by the life-principle infused into them by the necromancer who performs such acts consciously or by the medium who performs them unconsciously. To enable an astral form to continue to live after the death of the physical form, it must have attained spiritual life during the physical body's life."

"Surely," I said, "in every human being, the astral form contained within the physical body has life."

"True," she answered, "but not in every human being is it the centre of life and of consciousness. In ordinary mortals, the seat of life is in the blood contained in the veins and arteries of the physical form, and the astral form lives only, so to say, from the reflex of that physical life. In the Adept, the centre of life and consciousness has been established in the organism of their soul, clothed with the astral form, and is therefore self-conscious and independent of the physical body's life. I had already, during former incarnations, acquired that life and consciousness of the spirit. I was on the way to Adeptship before I was born in a lowly hut. During my childhood, I had spiritual intercourse with Adepts. However, I didn't know them intellectually because my intellectual activity, the result of my physical organization, wasn't sufficiently perfect to understand what my spirit perceived. But," she continued, "let us drop these metaphysical speculations, which I see fatigue your brain, and which become still more difficult of comprehension, as there is no rule without some exception. The laws of Nature are liable to produce endless varieties of modifications of action. Let us hear the history of our Sister Helen."

"Many thanks for your kindness in giving me so much information," I said, "but permit me to ask one more question. What were the voices you heard and the apparition you saw? Was it truly the archangel Michael who gave you your mission and aided you in your victories?"

"No," was the reply. "Angels don't interfere personally in mundane matters; spiritually developed humans are higher than them. It was the energy merger with one of our Brothers, who was formerly a great warrior and patriot, whose power entered within me and took the shape of a knight, representing the archangel for whom I always had a great veneration and whose image was foremost in my heart. But see..."

To my great astonishment, Layla suddenly became the luminous shape of a knight in brilliant armour, which shone like the sun so that I had to avert my eyes for fear of being blinded. The apparition disappeared within a few moments, and Layla returned in her previous form.

I had long observed the features of the other Lady-Adept, and it seemed as if I had seen her somewhere, perhaps in my dreams. Yes, I remember that when I was a mere child, I once had a vision, while in a state between sleeping and waking, when it seemed to me as if an angel or a superterrestrial being, clad in white and holding a white lily in her hand, were floating in the air over my head, extending the lily towards me. How often had I prayed in my heart to see that beautiful form again. If I wasn't mistaken, this lady was the form I had seen in my dream.

She was of exceeding great beauty. Her long, black, waving hair formed a strong contrast to her plain, white, and flowing robe, covering her form with graceful folds. Her tint was pale and delicate. Her profile was pure Greek; her dark eyes seemed to penetrate to the innermost centre of my soul and kindle there a fire of pure love and admiration.

"My life," said Helen, "was one of little importance. I was born in Saint Petersburg, and my father was an officer in the imperial army. He died while I was very young and left his family in great poverty. Besides the company of my mother, my relatives, and a teacher, there was nothing to attract me to Earth. My mind unfolded and revelled in superterrestrial joys. I loved poetry. I loved to look at the clouds sailing in the sky and to see images of their beauty. I communicated in spirit with the heroes of the past. But the development of my physical form couldn't keep in step with the unfoldment of the mind. Cold, starvation, and want to hasten its dissolution. After reaching my seventeenth year, I left my wasted, consumptive form and was kindly received by the Brothers."

Her plain and modest tale filled my heart with pity. "And was there no one," I said, "among your country people intelligent enough to perceive your genius and to give you support?"

"They erected a costly monument to my memory," she answered, "after my body had succumbed. A part of the money expended for it would have procured me the necessities to prolong my life. Those who knew me while living admired my poetry and my talents, but they were poor like myself. But let that pass. The conditions under which people live are the effects of previously acquired Karma. My poverty and suffering were my gain. I have cause to be well satisfied with my lot."[1]

While the lady spoke, I scanned her features. Was it really she who had appeared to me years ago in a dream? Was it she who waved that lily as if pronouncing a blessing? Was it the magnetic current which seemed to stream through that symbol into the depths of my heart and to call there a higher life into activity? Could that event have been a dream? Didn't it fill my whole being with happiness when it happened? Did its memory not remain deeply engraved in my heart when thousands of other dreams had faded away?

Helen rose and, reaching out through one of the open spaces between the pillars, she broke a white lily flower which grew close by the wall, which she gave to me, saying, "Keep this flower. It won't fade like a dream, and when you see it, you will know that I am not a product of hallucination."

I thanked her and begged her to remain my protector in the future, as she had been in the past. She answered: "We can only assist those who protect themselves. We can only influence those who are ready to receive our influence. We can only approach those who spiritually approach our own sphere. Love causes mutual attraction, and evil repulses. The pure will be attracted to the pure, the evil ones to that which is impure. To give presupposes the capacity to receive on the part of the one to receive. The sunlight is open to all, but not all can see it. The eternal fountain of truth is

---

[1] If you would like to know who Sister Helen was in her past life in Saint Petersburg, please visit radiantbooks.co/bonus.

inexhaustible and universal, but those who open their hearts to the sunshine of truth are few. Seek continually to rise above the sphere of selfishness, and you will be in the company of those who have thrown off their animal elements and live in the spirit."

As the lady finished speaking, another Adept approached the pavilion. He was of small stature but with a highly intellectual expression upon his face, which at once indicated that he must be a *Master*. His head was almost bald on the top and showed a most remarkable skull formation. On each side, however, there were grey locks of hair, and I immediately recognized in him one whose picture I had often seen and whose presence I had often felt and whom I will call Theodorus. He had been a great Adept and Rosicrucian during his earthly life; he had been a great physician and performed the most wonderful cures. He had been a great alchemist and knew the secret of the *Cross* and the *Rose*, of the *Red Lion* and the *White Eagle*.

As he entered, he announced that the Imperator had been called away to attend to some important affairs connected with politics on the mundane plane.[1] He jocularly remarked that he had gone to prevent a certain statesman from committing an act of imbecility, which would if he didn't succeed in stopping it, be productive of a great war. He was therefore deputed by the Imperator to show me the alchemical laboratory and to correct some of my misconceptions regarding alchemy. I was rather reluctant to leave the presence of the ladies, and I would have been willing to die at that moment to enable my soul to remain in their presence, but I couldn't with propriety decline the invitation. The ladies permitted me to retire, and I went with Theodorus into the monastery halls.

---

[1] In the 1930s, the Lord of Shambhala offered assistance to President Franklin D. Roosevelt through Helena Roerich, the last incarnation of Sister Helen. By accepting the guidance provided through her, Roosevelt was able to solve a number of problems facing the United States at the time. You can learn more about this in *The Secret World Government* by Helena Roerich.

VI

THE
ALCHEMICAL
LABORATORY

e went through a beautiful broad corridor, all along whose sides stood finely executed marble statues representing the gods and goddesses of antiquity and busts of the heroes of olden times.

"These statues," my companion remarked, "represent the elemental principles and powers of Nature, and they were thus personified by the ancients to bring the attributes of these principles within the conceptive power of the mind. None of the old Greeks and Romans, except the most ignorant, believed that Zeus, Pluto, Neptune, etc., were real personalities, nor did they worship them as such. They were merely symbols and personifications of formless powers. Likewise, every human's form and body is not the real individuality; it is merely a symbol and personification of their authentic character and attributes, a form of matter in which the thoughts of the real human have found their external expression. The ancients knew these things; it is only the modern wiseacres who mistake the external illusions for internal truths and the form for the principle. It is modern materialistic religion which has degraded the Universal Spirit into a limited being, and the great powers of Nature into Christian saints."

We entered a circular hall in the form of a temple. It had no windows but received its light from a cupola of clear glass. High over our heads, below the cupola, was a large interlaced double triangle made of gold and surrounded by a snake biting its tail. Directly under that symbol stood a round table with a white marble top, in the centre of which was a smaller representation of the figure above, executed in silver. The walls were ornamented with bookcases, in which were a great number of books on alchemy. At one side of the room, there was a kind of altar upon which stood a burning lamp. A couple of crucibles, a few bottles lying upon a side table, and some armchairs completed the room's furniture.

I looked around, expecting to see some furnaces, stoves, retorts, and other implements, such as are described in books on alchemy but could see none. My instructor, reading my thoughts, laughingly said: "Did you expect to find here an apothecary's shop? You made a mistake, my friend. All this array of bottles and pots,

furnaces, stoves, retorts, mortars, filters, strainers, distilling, puri-
fying, and refining apparatus, etc., described in books on alchemy,
is nothing but nonsense, written to mislead the selfish and vicious
and to prevent them from prying into mysteries which they are not
fit to receive. The true alchemist requires no ingredients for the
processes, such as could be bought in a chemist's shop. The alchemists find the required materials within their own organization.
The highest processes of alchemy require no mechanical labour;
they consist in the purification of the soul and in transforming an
animal-human into a divine being."

"But," I said, "didn't the ancient alchemists treat real metals
and transform them into others of a higher order?"

To this, Theodorus replied: "The invisible principles of which
the constitution of a human is made up are called *metals* because
they are more lasting and enduring than flesh and blood. The metals formed by thoughts and desires will continue to exist after the
perishing elements constituting the physical body have been dissolved. A human's animal principles are the base metals of which
their animal organization consists; they must be changed into nobler metals by transforming their vices into virtue until they pass
through *all* colours and turn into the gold of pure spirituality. To
accomplish this, the grossest elements in their form must die and
putrefy so that the light of the spirit penetrates through the hard
shell and calls the inner human into life and activity."

"Then," I said, "all those alchemical prescriptions which we
find in the books are only to be taken figuratively and have nothing
to do with material substances, such as salt, sulphur, mercury, etc."

"Not exactly so," answered the Adept. "No hard lines separate
the various kingdoms in Nature, and the actions of laws manifested
in one kingdom find their analogies in other kingdoms. The processes taking place in the spiritual planes are also taking place in the
astral and material planes, subject, of course, to such modifications
as are imposed by the conditions existing upon these planes. Nature isn't, as your scientists seem to believe, an agglomeration of
fundamentally different objects and elements; Nature is a whole,
and everything in the organism acts and is acted on by every other

thing contained therein. This is a fact that the ancient alchemists knew and which the modern chemists would do well to remember; for we find already in the book of *Zohar* the following passage, which I advise you to note down in your book so that you don't forget it:

> *Everything that exists upon the Earth has its ethereal counterpart above the Earth* (that is to say, in the inner realm)*, and there is nothing, however insignificant it may appear in the world, which is not depending on something higher* (or more interior)*; so that if the lower part acts, its presiding higher part reacts upon it.*

"The *Microcosm* of Human is a true counterpart, image, and representation of the great *Macrocosm* of Nature. In the former are contained all the powers, principles, forces, essences, and substances which are contained within the latter, from the supreme and divine spiritual principle, called *God*, down to the grossest state of the *Universal One Life*, in which it is called *Matter*. Those principles may be latent or active in either of the two organisms; they may exist merely germinally in a form, or they may be in a developed state."

"It has been taught by the ancients," I said, "that a human is a little world, constituted like the big world, which they inhabit."

"This is true," said the Adept, "but you should not merely know it as a theory but realize it. Within yourself is contained the universe with all its powers, heaven and hell, angels and devils, and all the kingdoms with their inhabitants, and you may call them into life at your pleasure. You are the god and creator within your own universe. You continually people that world with forms, coming into existence by your thoughts, and you infuse them with your life by the power of will. In each human being are contained germinally the essences which constitute the mineral, vegetable, animal, or human kingdom; in each human are contained principles which may be developed into a tiger, a snake, a hog, a dragon, a sage or a villain, into an angel or devil, into an Adept or a God.

Those elements which are made to grow and to be developed will become human and constitute their self. Look at the double interlaced triangle over your head; it represents the Macrocosm with all the forces, the interpenetration and union of Spirit and Matter, within the never-ending circle of eternity. Look at the smaller symbol upon the table before you; it represents the same elements within the constitution of Human. If you can bring the double interlaced triangles existing within your own self into exact harmony with those existing in the Universe, your powers will be the powers of Nature, and you will be able to guide and control by your reason and will the processes unconsciously, taking place within the realm of the latter."

I thought of the nature of the many different ingredients necessary to do an alchemical experiment and of how they must be mixed, but Theodorus perceived my thought and replied:

"The universal process, by which all the life processes take place, is the principle of Life. Those who can guide and control the power of life to do their will are alchemists. They can create new forms and increase the substance of those forms. The chemist creates nothing new; they merely form new combinations of the substances in their possession; the alchemist causes the substance to attract corresponding elements from the invisible storehouse in Nature and to increase. The chemist deals with matter in which the principle of life is inactive, that is, in which it manifests itself merely as mechanical or chemical energy; the alchemist deals with the principle of life and causes living forms to come into existence. The chemist may transform sulphur into invisible gas and cause that gas to become sulphur again, and the sulphur obtained at the end of the experiment will be just as much in quantity as it was at the beginning. Still, the gardener who puts a seed in the ground, and prepares the conditions necessary for that seed to grow into a tree, is an alchemist because they call something into existence which didn't exist ready-made in the seed. Out of one seed, they may thus obtain a thousand seeds of the same kind."

"But," I exclaimed, "it is said that the Rosicrucians possessed the power to turn iron, silver, or mercury into gold. Surely there is no gold in pure silver or mercury; how, then, could they cause something to grow which didn't exist?"

The Adept smiled and said: "It is as if through your lips speaks the learned ignorance of your modern civilization, which can't see the truth because it has created a mountain of misconceptions and scientific prejudices which now stand between itself and the truth. Let me tell you once more that *Nature is a Unity* and that, consequently, each particle of matter, even the smallest, is a part of Nature in which the possibilities of the whole are hidden. Each speck of dust may, under favourable conditions, develop into a universe where all the elements existing in Nature can be found. The reason why your scientists are unable to comprehend this truth is that their fundamental doctrines about the constitution of matter and energy are entirely wrong. Your Dualism in theology has been the cause of untold misery, creating a continual quarrel between God and the Devil; your Polytheism in science blinds the eyes and obstructs the judgement of the learned and keeps them in ignorance. What do you know about the attributes of primordial matter? What do you know about the difference between matter and force? All the so-called simple substances known to your science are originally grown out of primordial matter. But this primordial matter is a Unity; it is only *One*.

"Consequently, each particle of this primordial matter must be able to grow under certain conditions into gold, under other conditions to produce iron, under others mercury, etc. This is what the ancient alchemists meant when they said that each of the seven metals contains the seeds of the other seven. They also taught that to transmute one body into another, the body to be transmuted would have to be reduced first into its *Prima Materia*.

"But," he continued, "I see that you are anxious to have the truth of these doctrines demonstrated by an experiment; let us then see whether it is possible to make gold grow out of its *seed*."

VII

THE SECRET
OF ALCHEMY

ithout rising from the big armchair in which Theodorus was seated, he then directed me to take one of the crucibles upon the table, to see that it was empty, and to put it upon a tripod over the flame burning upon the altar. I did as directed. He then said: "Now take some of the silver pieces which you have in your pocket and throw them into the crucible." I took seven coins and did as he said. After a few minutes, they began to melt, and, as I saw the silver in the crucible had become fluid, I told the Adept that it was molten. He then indicated a small bottle containing some red powder, which stood upon the table, and requested me to take some of that red powder and throw it into the crucible. There was a little silver spoon lying upon the table, and with this, I took what seemed to be about one or two grains of the red powder from the bottle and was going to throw it into the crucible, but Theodorus stopped me, saying that this was too much powder, and it shouldn't be wasted. He told me to throw the powder back into the bottle and wipe the spoon with a piece of paper, and then throw it into the crucible. The quantity of powder which adhered to the spoon after I had returned the former to the bottle was so little as to be hardly visible; nevertheless, I did as he told me and threw the little piece of paper upon the molten silver. Immediately the paper burned, and the molten metal began to foam and rise so that I was afraid it would run over the sides of the crucible. Still, each bubble burst as it reached the top and exhibited various beautiful colours.

This play lasted for about fifteen minutes when the boiling ceased, and the foaming mass sank back to the bottom of the crucible. Theodorus noticed that it had become quiet; he directed me to take the crucible from the fire and to pour the contents upon a marble slab. I did as he told me, and directly the mass became solid and appeared to be the finest gold.

"Take this gold with you," said Theodorus, "and let it be examined so that you will be convinced that you have not been the victim of a hallucination."

I was very much astonished, and I thought how much our people would give to become acquainted with the secret of this red powder. I desired to ask the Adept how this powder could be prepared, but I didn't dare to ask the question aloud because I was afraid that Theodorus would think I desired to know the secret to enrich myself. But the Adept saw my thought and said:

"The secret of how this red powder is prepared cannot be explained until humanity becomes more spiritual; because it is a secret which cannot be merely theoretically explained but whose knowledge must be practically acquired. How can we teach humankind to employ powers they don't possess and of which they don't even know existed? Nevertheless, the germs of these powers are contained in a latent condition within the organism of every human being.

"It would be foolish to suppose that gold could be made out of any other substance than gold, but every substance contains the germ of gold in its own primordial matter.

"In the alchemical laboratory of Nature, iron-pyrites and other substances produce gold in the course of ages because the principle of gold contained in their primordial element grows by the action of the life-principle of Nature and becomes visible gold. This process, which may require unconscious Nature millions of years to accomplish, can be accomplished by Nature in a few minutes if her will-power is guided by the spiritual consciousness and intelligence of the Adept. It is as impossible to make gold grow out of anything containing no gold as it is impossible to make an apple tree grow out of a cherry stone. But if we wish to see an apple tree grow out of a seed, we don't insert it in a hole bored into a rock but select a proper piece of soil where it can grow with the aid of warmth and moisture. Likewise, if we desire to grow gold out of the 'seed' or *principle* of gold, we must add the proper soil that it requires. This 'soil' is furnished by the red powder, which contains the life-principle for producing gold. Know that there is no 'dead' substance in the Universe and that even a stone or a metal contains life in a latent form. If the life-principle within such a substance becomes active, this substance will begin to form and produce the various colours you saw in the crucible. If the mass were cold and solid, the element of life would be slow to penetrate below the metal's surface. Nevertheless, the transmutation would gradually take place. But in the molten mass, the life-giving substance becomes thoroughly mixed with the metal, ebullition takes place, and the transmutation is quickly performed.

"Why should growth and development and transmutation of the form be possible only in the vegetable and animal kingdom? It is equally possible in the mineral kingdom; the only difference is that in the former, it takes place within a sufficiently short period to come within human observation. While in the latter, these processes take place very slowly, and many generations may pass away before any progress in the growth of metals can be observed.

"The seed for the production of plants grows in the plants themselves; the seed for the production of animals grows in the animals; the 'seed' for the production of metals rests in the metals. It isn't sufficient merely to melt gold, to make it grow; it must be reduced to what the alchemists call *Water*, which means its primordial matter. This is done by adding the red powder, of which an almost imperceptible quantity is sufficient to cause the growth of a great quantity of gold. The few atoms of powder which you used were enough and to spare to transmute your silver, as you will see if you now examine your gold, which hasn't absorbed all of the red powder which adhered to the paper."

I looked at the gold, which had now become cold enough to be handled, and, indeed, upon its surface, there were some little red pearls like rubies, which seemed to indicate that they were parts of the red powder which had not been absorbed by the molten mass.

"This red powder," Theodorus continued, "is the celebrated *Red Lion* of the Alchemists. Some call it *Sulphur*, others call it *Mercury*, and some call it *Salt*. It is, indeed, each of those three, one as well as the other, for the three form a Trinity in a Unity, which is inseparable and cannot be divided."

"Master!" I exclaimed, "teach me this secret, and I promise you that I will never use the knowledge obtained for any selfish purpose. I have learned enough of occultism to know that worldly possessions and riches are useless for the purpose of spiritual development and that they are, in truth, the greatest obstacles which can be put in the way of those who desire to progress. I only desire to know the truth for the sake of the truth and not to obtain any selfish advantage. Teach me these secrets, and I will forget my self and devote my life to benefit the Universal Brotherhood of Humanity."

"Very well," answered the Adept. "I will do all I can to show you the way, but you must do your own walking. To teach you the secret of how to make gold is identical to teaching you all the secrets of the constitution of Nature and of its counterpart, the microcosm of humans. This cannot be done in a few hours or within a few days, and it would be against the rules of our order to retain you here longer than after sunset. But to enable you to study this science of alchemy, I will lend you a book you may read and study. If you keep your intuitional faculties open and your mind unclouded, I will be invisibly near you and assist you in understanding the meaning of the secret symbols contained therein."

With these words, Theodorus handed me a book containing several coloured plates with symbols and signs. It was an old book, and its title was *The Secret Symbols of the Rosicrucians of the Sixteenth and Seventeenth Centuries.*

"The size of the book," continued the Adept, "renders it rather inconvenient to carry on your descent from the mountain, but I will send it to your hotel in the village, where you will find it on your arrival."

I thanked the Adept and looked once more at the mysterious book. I glanced at the titles of the pages and saw that they treated the greatest of mysteries, of the Macrocosm and Microcosm, of Time and Eternity, of Occult Numbers, the Four Elements, the Trinity of All, of Regeneration, Alchemy, Philosophy, and Kabbalah; it was indeed a book on *Universal Science.*

"If you practically understand the contents of this book," said Theodorus, "you won't merely know how to produce gold out of the baser metals, which is one of the lowest, most insignificant, and comparatively worthless parts of our art, but you will know the mystery of the Rose and the Cross; you will know how to come into possession of the *Philosopher's Stone* and the *Universal Panacea,* which renders those who possess it immortal. You will then

not merely know how to direct the processes of life to make pearls
and diamonds and precious stones grow, but you will know how
to make a human out of an animal and a god out of a human. This
last alchemical process is the one thing which is needed, and in
comparison, all other arts are merely playthings for children. What
will it serve us to run after illusions, which will vanish in time, if
we can obtain within ourselves that which is eternal and real?"

I asked the Adept whether I would be permitted to show that
book to others or to have it copied and printed; upon which he
replied:

"There are at present few people in the world who would be
able to comprehend this book to its fullest extent, but there are
some who desire to know the truth, and for the sake of these few,
you may risk throwing pearls before the swine. The symbols contained in these pages must be not merely seen and studied with
the intellect; they must also be grasped by the spirit. To make this
plain, know that each occult symbol and sign, from a mere point
up to the double-interlaced Triangle to the Rose and the Cross,
has three significations. The first is the exoteric meaning, which
is easily understood; the second is the esoteric or secret signification, which may be intellectually explained; the deepest and most
mysterious one is the third, the spiritual meaning, which cannot be
explained, but which must be practically experienced by the spirit.
This practical, internal experience is arrived at by the power of intuition, or the faculty by which the spirit often feels the presence
of things one cannot see with the bodily senses and, therefore, not
understand intellectually as long as one has no spiritual power. If
a person once feels interior things with their heart, sees them by
their internal sight, and understands their attributes through their
intellect, such a person has become illuminated and is practically
an Adept.

"As the number *Three* grows out of the *One*, likewise the *Seven*
grows out of the *Three*; because by a combination of three numbers
or letters four complications arise, forming with the original Three
the number Seven; and thus there are not merely three, but seven
explanations of each symbol. You see, therefore, that the matter is

very complicated and requires deep study. Nor would it benefit you if I were to explain to you all the various meanings of these symbols, for to learn such explanations from another doesn't necessarily convey real knowledge but is often merely a matter of stuffing the memory with the opinions of another. Such knowledge is of the kind which is acquired in your colleges and universities, and we want none of it. Self is the human being. That which they find out by their own experience, that they *know*, and nothing more.

"You must learn to realize that you are a symbol. These symbols represent the mysteries of the Universe and of humans. You are that Universe, the human, and these things represent yourself. What good would the explanations do to you if you don't realize they are true?"

"But," I replied, "if this is so, it will be useless to read any such books."

"Those who know these things themselves," said Theodorus, "don't need them, and those who do need them don't understand them. Books of that kind are like mirrors in which one sees the things reflected which exist within them. A monkey stands before a looking-glass and sees its own image but thinks it is another monkey aping its motions. If you know the contents of a book, describing a truth, you only know the description but not the very truth itself. You may know the contents of the Bible by heart from beginning to end, together with all the commentaries, and still not realize the truth of one iota of it.

"When I was an inhabitant of your world, I had many a hard rub with your doctors of medicine and divinity because they lived upon the ignorance of the people. The more I enlightened the latter, the less flattering grew the bread-and-butter prospects of the former. I usually found that the more learned your doctors were, the more did they lose their own common sense. I live here in peace and care little about their disputations and argumentations, but I occasionally glance at the world, and I don't see much change for the better."

"Nevertheless," I said, "you will agree that science has made a great deal of progress since those days?"

"True," he answered, "it has progressed in some things and retrograded in others. Science has made many inventions to increase the physical comforts of humanity and to gratify their desires. Still, in proportion, as people's desires have been gratified, they have also grown, and new necessities have been created. Many of your most useful inventions, however, have not been made with the help but rather despite the opposition of your professional scientists. But of what use are all these scientific attainments for the eternal well-being of personality? They are made for the comfort of the physical form, and their usefulness ceases when the physical form ceases to exist. These attainments would be all right if people didn't waste all their time enjoying them, thereby neglecting the development of the *metals*, which will last far longer than the physical form.

"Moreover, if the psychical human faculties were developed, many of your most useful inventions would be perfectly useless; they would be displaced by far better methods, in the same sense as bows and arrows have become useless since the invention of gunpowder and guns. You are very proud of your railroads and telegraphs, but of what use are they to someone who can travel with the velocity of thought from one place to another, however distant that place may be. Learn to chain the elemental spirits of Nature to the chariot of your science, and you may mount like an eagle and ride through the air."

"I should be very glad," I said, "if you would inform me how a person can travel with the velocity of thought from one place to another. It seems that the weight of the physical body would present an insurmountable impediment."

"Neither would psychically developed human beings need to take that cumbrous form along on such travels," answered Theodorus. "What or who is a human being? Are they that semi-animal mechanism, which eats, drinks, and walks, and wastes nearly half of its life in unconscious sleep; that mass of bones and muscles, of blood and sensitive nerves, which hinders the free movements of the spirit who is chained to it; or is it that invisible something which thinks and feels, and knows that it exists?"

I said: "Undoubtedly, the real human is our thinking principle."

"If you admit this," answered the Adept, "you will also agree that the real human is in that place and locality wherein they think and perceive. In other words, they are where their consciousness exists. Thinking is a faculty of the mind and not the physical body. It is not my brain which thinks, but I do my thinking using my brain. Wherever our mind exercises that faculty, there is our true habitation; whether our physical form is there, too, is a circumstance which need not concern us any more than it would concern us to carry a warm and heavy coat which we are accustomed to wearing in winter along with us while we are making a summer excursion. Thinking is a faculty of the mind, and Mind is universal. If we learn to think independently of our physical brain, we may as well exercise that faculty in one place of the Universe as in another, without taking our physical body along."

"But," I asked, "how can a universal and therefore unorganized principle think without using for that purpose an organized brain?"

"O short-sighted mortal!" exclaimed Theodorus, smiling. "Who says that the Universal Mind is without an organization? Who has so little judgement as to suppose that the highest organized living and conscious principle in the Universe is without an organization, if even the inferior kingdoms upon the face of the Earth, such as crystal, plant, and animal, can't exist without an organization? Surely the air does not think; it has no firm organization, but the Universal Mind is not air, nor is it empty space; it has nothing in common with either, except its being everywhere present. It is the highest organized principle in the Universe.

"Inferior humans, in whom the consciousness of higher spiritual self hasn't awakened, cannot think without the physical brain; they cannot experience a consciousness they don't yet possess; they can't exercise a faculty which is merely latent within their organization. But the one who has awakened to the consciousness of their higher self, whose life has been concentrated into their higher principles, which exist independently of the physical form, constitutes a *spiritual* centre of consciousness, which doesn't require the physical brain to think, any more than you require the use of your

hands and feet for the purpose of thinking. If a person in a som-
nambulic condition travels in spirit to a distant place and reports
what they have seen there, and their observations are afterwards
verified, must we not conclude that they have been at that place,
and would it be reasonable to suppose that they have taken their
physical brain with them and left their empty skull behind? How
absurd is such an idea, but verily its absurdity doesn't surpass that
of your suggestion that the Universal Mind is without an organization."

I was somewhat confused at having inconsiderately expressed
an opinion about a subject I couldn't know anything about. The
Adept, noticing my regret, continued mildly: "If you desire to
know the organization of Nature, study your own constitution,
not merely in its physical, anatomical, and physiological aspect,
but especially in its psychological aspect. Study what may be called
the physiology of your soul. If your foot were not an organized substance intimately connected with your brain through the nerves
and the spinal cord, you would never be able to feel any sensation.
Your foot might be burned or amputated, and you wouldn't be
aware of it unless you saw its destruction or become otherwise conscious of its loss. You don't think with your foot. You think with
your brain. Or, to express it more correctly, you think by means of
your brain. But if you were more spiritually developed, you would
be able to sink your thought and consciousness from your brain
down into your feet or into any other part of your body and, so
to say, live in that part and be entirely unconscious of any other
part. It has already come to the comprehension of some of your
more advanced scientists that sensation and consciousness may
be withdrawn from any part of the body, either by the will and
imagination of the person undertaking the experiment or by the
aid of the will and imagination of a magnetizer or mesmerizer. In
the same manner, the opposite thing can be done, and someone
may concentrate, so to say, in any part of their own organism or
in any part of the great organism of Nature with which they are
intimately and inseparably, although invisibly, connected.

"Someone who believes they exist independently of Nature and separated from it labours under a great illusion. The fundamental doctrine of occultism is that Nature is only one, that all beings in Nature are intimately connected, and that everything in Nature acts upon every other thing therein. The feeling of isolation and separateness existing in individuals is only caused by the illusion of form. A human being's form isn't the inner self; it is merely a state of matter in which they exist for the time being and is continually subject to change. It may be compared to an image in a mirror in which an individual's character is imperfectly reflected. Although it differs from the image in a mirror in so far as it is temporarily endowed or infused with life, sensation, and consciousness, it is nothing more than an image. For life, sensation and consciousness don't belong to the form; they are functions of the invisible. But a real human — who forms a part of the invisible organism of Nature, and whose mind is a part of the Universal Mind, and who, therefore, if they once realize their true character and learn to know their own powers — may concentrate their consciousness in any place, within or beyond their physical form, and see, feel, and understand what takes place in such a locality."

"These ideas," I said, "are so grand that I'm not yet fully able to grasp them, but I fear that they will never be accepted by our scientists, who cannot see beyond the narrow systems they have created."

"True," answered the Adept; "they won't be accepted or understood by our present generation of scientists. But they will be known in the future to those who are not merely learned but wise, as they were known to the wise men and women of the past. Ignorance and self-conceit are twins, and it flatters one's vanity to believe that they are something superior to and different from the rest. The more someone is learned in superficial science, the more they believe in their own imaginary superiority and separateness. The consciousness of the great majority of intelligent people in our intellectual age is nearly all concentrated within their brains; they live, so to say, entirely in the top storey of their houses. But the brain isn't the most important part. The centre of life is the heart, and if consciousness doesn't reside in the centre of life, it will become separate from life and finally cease to exist. Let those who desire to develop spiritually attempt to think with their hearts instead of continually studying with their brains. Let them attempt to sink day after day their power of thought down to the centre of life in the heart until their consciousness is firmly established there. At first, they will see nothing but darkness; but if they persevere in their efforts, they will behold a light at that centre which illuminates the mind. This inextinguishable light will send its rays to the brain and carry them as far as the stars, and in it, they may see the past, the present, and the future.

"The greatest mysteries in Nature are by no means difficult to understand if we only prefer to look at them instead of our own illusions. The grandest ideas are easy to grasp if we merely prefer to grasp them instead of holding on to those we have created. Our mind is like a mirror in which the ideas floating in the Universal Mind are reflected, comparable to a tranquil lake in which you may see the true images of the passing clouds. If the lake's surface is disturbed, the images become distorted. If the water becomes muddy, the reflections cease altogether. Likewise, if the mind is in a tranquil state and clear of foreign elements, the person will reflect on the grandest and noblest ideas existing within the world of the mind. If we desire to think reasonably, we should allow Reason to do its thinking within our brain. Still, if we attempt to be wiser than Reason, our mind becomes filled with our own illusions and those we have acquired from others, and we cannot see the truth as it is, but we see it as we imagine it to be.

"This truth you will find symbolically or allegorically represented in all the world's principal mythologies and religious systems. It is the old story of the *Fall of Man*. As long as humanity remained in a state of purity — that is to say, as long as will and imagination were identical to the will and the imagination of the spiritual power acting within Nature — they knew the truth and were all-powerful. But when they began to think and to imagine in a way different from that universal power, they lost sight of the truth and could see only their own illusions. If a person wants to see the truth again, they must give up their own way of thinking and reasoning and let Reason will and think in them. But you may as well ask a miser to give up the treasure which they have collected and hoarded during a lifetime as to ask a modern scientist or philosopher to give up their own way of thinking. I see in your heart a desire to establish a reasonable society; but let me warn you that if you attempt to accomplish this by appealing to those who are clever and cunning, vainglorious and proud of their own attainments, full of ambition and anxious to come into possession of occult or magical powers to gratify their scientific curiosity or to employ them for the fulfilment of some selfish desire, you will certainly fail; for it is written: 'Whosoever hath, to him shall be given, and he shall have more in abundance, but whosoever hath not, from him shall be taken away even that he hath.'"

"I know that quotation," I answered, "but its meaning isn't quite clear to me."

"It means," replied Theodorus, "that to one with a love of wisdom in their heart, abundant light will be given; but one who is filled with selfish desires will lose even what little understanding they have."

"I acknowledge," I said, "that I have been thinking of finding means to establish such a society, or a school for spiritual development, where those who desire to progress might be able to spend their energies for the purpose of that which is useful and lasting, instead of being forced to run after the illusions of the world. I have been mentally seeking a place in solitude where the members of such a society might lead an interior life. I should like to establish a theosophical monastery where we could live like you, surrounded by all the grandeur, sublimity, and stillness of Nature, escape the servitude of fashionable society, and step on the path to Adeptship. But surely, I couldn't think of selecting our members from the ranks of the uneducated and ignorant."

"Select them among those who are pure and virtuous," answered Theodorus, "and your choice will be well made. Choose those who have overcome preconceived opinions and prejudices; select them among those who have no desire to obtain knowledge for their own personal benefit and don't wish to shine but to let the light grow within themselves. Such persons are very rare, but if you find any, and if they join you in your efforts, you will soon have the most enlightened society in the world. That which is today called *learning and education* is merely a very laborious method of acquiring a little superficial knowledge which humankind is forced to adopt because they don't know how to develop their spiritual faculties. If this method were taught and practised, real knowledge would soon occupy the place of mere learning, certainty the place of belief, conviction the place of opinion, and true faith the place of creed. If every inhabitant of your proposed monastery had no way of willing and imagining of their own, but if they all were living mirrors in which Divine Wisdom is reflected without any adulteration, such a monastery would be the greatest ornament of the world. Such centres of spiritual intelligence would be like suns of the first magnitude on the mental horizon of the world. One such centre would be sufficient to illuminate the world with its wisdom and to send its intellectual rays to the utmost limits of the planet."

"And what is to hinder the establishment of such a centre of intelligence?" I asked.

"Nothing but human imperfections and the abundance of selfish desires," answered the Adept. "There are two sources from which the obstacles arise that are in the way of those who desire to attain self-knowledge and immortality. One class of obstacles arises from the interior self, the other from the external conditions in which one lives. The internal obstacles are caused by one's acquired scientific or theological prejudices and misconceptions regarding the human constitution and by the living elemental forces active within the animal principle in their constitution. As they are fed and grow strong by external influences, they manifest themselves in various ways, producing animal impulses. Combined with intellectual acquirements, they grow into the more dangerous class of vices, such as ambition, vanity, greed, intolerance, selfishness, etc. Each of these animal elements, or *Elementals*, may grow into an intellectual but unreasonable being and finally constitute the

Ego. A human being may have many such *Egos* until perhaps one of these overmasters the others and becomes a king in the realm of their soul. Each of these *Egos* absorbs a share of the life and consciousness of the person whose soul exists and may even occupy all space within their intellectual sphere to paralyse reason or drive it away. The world is crowded with intellectual or semi-intellectual Elementals in human shape, in whom reason has been paralysed to a greater or lesser extent. You see them every day in the streets, in the pulpit, in the forum, in the halls of learning, as well as in the marketplace. A person's principal object in life should be to keep the realm of their mind free from such intruders so that the king Reason may rule therein without being impeded. Their duty is to fight the Herculean battle with those animal and intellectual Elementals so that they will become servants of the king and not his masters. Can this be accomplished if all our energies are continually employed on the outward plane; if we are never at home within ourselves; if we are continually engaged with the illusions of life, either in the pursuit of sensual gratification or entirely absorbed in the so-called intellectual pursuits, which tend to give us knowledge of outward things but convey no knowledge of self? Can we expect to accumulate our energy and employ it at the centre within ourselves if we continually spend it at the periphery? Can we hope to be able to waste all our power and, at the same time, be able to retain it? An affirmative answer would be as irrational as unscientific."

VIII

THE WISDOM
OF THE SAGES

It would be too tedious to some of our readers if I were to report all the instructions given to me by my kind guide Theodorus, who, for all I know, may have been known as the celebrated Theophrastus Paracelsus during his life in the physical body. I don't, however, feel justified in omitting to tell what he said about the importance of practising self-control and developing firmness of character and individuality. Previously to my visit to the Rosicrucian convent, attempts had been made to force me to believe that occultism and mysticism were things only for dreamers, adapted to persons living continually in the clouds, enjoying their superstitions and vagaries by building castles in the air. But now, I have become more convinced that self-reliance is a most necessary quality for a disciple of this sacred science and that no science can be more exact than the one based upon our own spiritual knowledge and realized within our soul. Thus Theodorus said:

"A power to become strong at a centre must be directed towards the centre. For it is only by resistance it can accumulate and become strong. A monarch who goes away from their kingdom and leaves it without protection may find other rulers when they attempt to return. To become conquerors over Nature, we must fight our battles and not wait until Nature fights them for us. The more the animal elements within our constitution are stimulated into life and activity by the temptations coming from the external world through the avenues of the senses, the hotter will be the battle, and the stronger our reason will grow if we successfully resist. This is the battle that the great Gautama Buddha fought and from which he came out victorious because he was overshadowed by the *Bo-Tree* of Wisdom.

"I will attempt to give you a rational and scientific explanation of the effects of inward concentration of mind and introspection; and, that you may not think I am revealing secrets which ought not to be revealed to the uninitiated, I refer you to the books of the great Greek philosopher Plotinus who revealed them long ago, but whose ideas are still far beyond the grasp and understanding of your modern lights of wisdom.

"According to that philosopher, there exists nothing in the Universe but *God*; but if this word doesn't please someone, because it has for ages been subject to misconceptions, and because, if we speak of God, the people will insist in imagining that we are referring to an external and personal god, which is an absurdity because no place can be found in Nature for such a god — let us call it the *Real*?

"According to Plotinus, nothing has any real existence, but the Real, and all the phenomena in this Universe are merely illusions created by the internal activity of the Real. No one can see their own face without the aid of a mirror. Likewise, the Real, when it awakes from its sleep after the great *Pralaya*, cannot see itself without the aid of a mirror. There is no other substance but that which belongs to the Real to serve as a mirror. And therefore, the Real, so to say, steps out of its own centre and looks within itself, and thus an intellectual activity is created by which the Real perceives the images existing within its own substance. This activity going from the periphery towards the centre is called the *Universal Mind*.

"The teachings of the sages say that the Universal Spirit called the world into existence by the power of His own Will. All great religions speak of a Divine Triunity, according to Christianity, called the Father, the Son, and the Holy Ghost. The will or intention is the Father, the thought or idea is the Son, and the creative power of the Father acting through the Son is the Holy Ghost. By this power, the thoughts of the Father become manifest, and thus visible objective worlds are called into existence."

"But," I said, "where does the Father find the material or substance to render these thoughts visible and objective?"

"Within Himself," answered my guide, and, looking at me as if to make sure that I understood what he said, he continued: "*Allah il Allah*, says the Mohammedan; God is God, and there is nothing beside Him. He is the All; matter and motion and space, consciousness, intelligence, wisdom, spirit, substance, energy, darkness, and light. The worlds are His outspoken Will, but there is nothing outside of Himself which He cannot create. He is the All, including and penetrating everything. Thus everything exists within Him, who is the life and soul of all things. In Him, we live and move and have our being, and without Him, we are nothing.

"A human is the god and creator of their own little world, and therefore similar processes take place if a person by the power of introspection directs their thoughts towards their own centre of consciousness existing in their *heart*, and thus attempts to see what is going on within themselves. Now this activity going towards the centre could never have created an external world because the external world exists, so to say, on the periphery, and requires a centrifugal power to call it into existence. The intellectual activity of the Universal Mind is a centripetal power and couldn't, therefore, act from the centre towards the periphery. But you know that every action is followed by a reaction. The centripetal power finding resistance at the centre returns and evolves a centripetal activity, and this centripetal power is called the *Soul*. This *soul-energy* is the medium between the centre and the periphery, between Spirit and Matter, between the Creator and His creations, between God and Nature, or whatever names you may choose to give to it. The *Soul* is the product of the centrifugal activity of the Universal Will, put into action by the centripetal activity of the Universal Imagination.

"If these plain facts, expressed in plain language, without any scientific jargon, without circumlocutions, philosophical intricacies, and modern gibberish, are comprehensible to you, all you have to do is to apply it to human beings, who are the microcosmic counterpart of the great macrocosm of Nature. If you direct the power of your mind inwardly towards your centre, instead of letting it fly off into the external sensual world, the resistance that it finds at the centre will cause a reaction, and the stronger the centripetal power which you apply, the stronger will be the centrifugal power created; in other words, the stronger will your *Soul* become, and, as it grows strong, it is invisible, but nevertheless material substance will penetrate your physical, visible body, and serve to transform it into a higher kind of matter. Thus you may, in the end, become all *Soul* and have no gross physical body. But long before that time arrives, you will be able to act upon the matter by the power of your soul, cure your own bodily ills and those of other people, and do many wonderful things, even at distances far away from your visible form; for the activity of the soul is not limited by the circumference of the physical form but radiates far into the sphere of the Universal Mind."

I told Theodorus that these ideas were too grand and new to me to be grasped immediately but that I would attempt to remember them and meditate about them in the future.

"You will do well if you do so," said the Adept, "and I will take care that they remain in your memory."

"If the sages' doctrines are true," I replied, "it would seem that the vast majority of our thinkers are continually thinking the wrong way; because they are engaged all their lives in prying into the manifestations of life on the outward plane, and don't seem to care a straw about what is taking place within the inner life of the soul."

"Therefore," answered Theodorus, "they will perish with their illusions, and the Bible is right in saying that the ways of the worldly wise are foolishness in the eyes of the Eternal.

"What will it serve you if your head is full of intellectual rubbish and speculations about the details of the phenomenal illusions of life, and you become a senile imbecile in your old age? What will it serve you, roaming about the world and gratifying your curiosity in regard to its details, when, after that world has vanished, they forever disappear from your memory? Perhaps it would be better for the learned if they knew less about scientific theories and had more practical self-knowledge. It would be better to have fewer scientific speculations and more spiritual power. If they were to employ, for instance, their time and energy for developing the spiritual power of clairvoyance instead of spending it on finding out the habits of some species of African monkeys, they would fare better by it. If they were to obtain the power to heal the sick by the touch of their hands, instead of seeking new methods to poison humanity by inoculations of injurious substances, humanity would be the gainer. There are thousands of people who work hard all their lives without accomplishing anything really useful or enduring. Thousands labour intellectually or mechanically to perform work which had better be left undone. There are vastly more people engaged in undermining and destroying the population's health than in curing its ills. More engaged in teaching error than the truth, and more trying to find that which is worthless than that of value. They live, and will perish, in the externals; they run after money, and the money will remain while they perish and die.

"The obstacles which arise from the external world are intimately connected with those from the inner world and cannot be separated; because external temptations create inward desires, and inward desires call for external means for gratification. Still, many people don't crave the illusions of life but don't have the strength to resist them. Many have a desire to develop spiritually and to gain immortality. Still, they believe themselves forced by external circumstances, which they dare not resist, to employ all of their time and energy to attain worthless things instead of using their strength to dive down into the depths of the soul to search for the priceless pearl of wisdom. Thousands of people haven't the moral courage to break loose from social customs, ridiculous habits, and foolish usages, which they inwardly abhor, but to which they nevertheless submit because these are customs and habits to act against, which is considered to be a social crime. Thus thousands sacrifice their immortality to the stupid goddess of fashion.

"Who dares to break loose from the bondage imposed upon them by the fashion which currently dominates religious thought and to exchange for it the freedom of eternal life? Who dares to face the calumny and the contempt of the ignorant to obtain in its place the applause of the wise? Who has the courage to incur the sneers of the imbecile, the ridicule of the ignorant, the laughter of the fool, and gain thereby a light of whose existence those who live in eternal darkness know nothing? But the vast majority drown the voice of reason by the speculating power of the intellect. Rather than have their vanity suffer, they allow the spirit to starve; rather than be crucified and resurrected into immortal life, they submit to the galling chain; they lose their appreciation of liberty and, becoming used to their chains, begin to love them and impose them upon others; thus proving true the saying of the poet:

It is the curse of every evil act,
That it forever must give birth to evil.

"I am not a believer in the total depravity of human nature; I know that humankind's animal principles, on account of their inherent, instinctive efforts for the preservation of their existence, are opposed to the development of their higher principles because the life of the higher involves the death of the lower; but I also know that in each human being is contained a power for good, which may be made to develop if the proper conditions are given. There are elements of good and evil in everyone, and it depends which class we desire to develop. From a cherry stone, nothing can grow but a cherry tree, from a thistle seed nothing else than a thistle; but a human being is a constellation of powers in which all kinds of seeds are contained; you may make them grow to be a hog or a tiger, an angel or a devil, a sage or a fool, according to your own pleasure.

"The continual rush after more money, more comfort, more pleasure, after we already possess all we require, which characterizes our present civilization, isn't necessarily a sign of greed, viciousness, and moral depravity; but it is rather caused by the instinctive impulse, inherent in the human constitution, to reach something higher and better, which expresses itself on the physical plane. Humans intuitively know that, no matter how wealthy or famous they may be, they have not yet reached a state in which they will be contented to rest; they know they must still keep on striving for something, but they don't know what that something is. Not knowing the higher life, they strive for more of those things which the lower life affords and thus waste their energies on the attainment of useless things. Thus we may see a bug or a butterfly falling into a lake and, in its vain efforts to save itself from drowning, swimming away from the shore because it doesn't know in which direction the means for salvation exist. Thus the curse of the world and the root of all evil is ignorance. The curse of humankind is the ignorance of their essential nature and final destiny. The efforts of a true system of religion and science ought to be, above all, to remove this stupidity.

"But it is also true that ignorance and conceit are closely connected and that the ignorant hate someone wiser than themselves. If one person, knowing more about the requirements of their nature and desirous of employing their energies for the attainment of a higher state, were to dare to assert their man- or womanhood and to rebel against the chains of fashion, could they continue to live unmolested in their community? And if they were to emigrate to another, wouldn't they be exposed there to the same troubles? They would still come in contact with others who hated the light because they were educated in darkness, who would misunderstand them, suspect their motives, persecute them, and woe to those with any human failings upon which the snake of slander could fasten its poison fangs. Wherever darkness exists, there exists abhorrence of light. Wherever an ignorant human enters, their imperfections enter. Wherever ignorance resides, there is an entourage of suspicion, envy, and fear. Wouldn't it be more within the scope of true science to enlighten humankind about their true nature than to invent theories regarding the causes of phenomena they don't know and can't prevent?

"That which is almost impossible to accomplish by the unaided efforts of a single individual may often easily be accomplished by the cooperation of many. This law seems to prevail in all departments of Nature. If a sufficient number of people were determined to retire from the harlequin stage of the world and to turn away from the tomfooleries of a fashionable existence, they might, if they could harmonize with each other, form a power sufficiently strong to repel the attacks of the monster which would devour them all if they were separated and unaided by each other. Those who are not yet progressed far on the ladder of evolution need those who are upon a higher step to assist them on their upward way, and the higher ones, to some extent, need the lower for their support, in the same sense as a rock needs solid ground to rest upon and maintain its position.

"There have been at previous times, as there are now, numerous people who became convinced that there is a higher and inner life and desired to surround themselves with such conditions as were most favourable for its attainment. Such people were not only found in Christian countries but also among the 'heathen.' And thousands of years ago, lamaseries and lodges, orders, monasteries, convents, and refuges were established, where people might strive to attain a higher life unimpeded by the aggressions and annoyances of the external world of illusions. Their original purpose was, beyond doubt, very commendable. If, over time, many such institutions have become degraded and lost their original character — instead of being places for the performance of the noblest and most difficult kind of labour but instead become places of refuge for the indolent, idle, and superstitious — it is not the fault of that principle that first caused such institutions to be organized. However, it is the consequence of losing the knowledge of humans' true nature, powers, and destiny. With the loss of that knowledge, the means for attaining the original aim were naturally lost and forgotten.

"Such a degradation took place in Europe, especially during and after the Middle Ages, when, enriched by robberies and endowed by dying thieves who wanted to buy salvation, the clergy amassed great wealth and lived a luxurious life, feasting on the fat of the land. They then knew nothing more of the conditions of a higher existence; they became centres of attraction for the hypocrite and the idle. They passed away their idle hours in apparently pious amusements and striving to gain more material wealth. Instead of being centres from which blessings should spread over the country, they became a plague to the land. They robbed the rich, and, vampire-like, they sucked the last drop of blood out of the poor. They continued in this manner until the cup of their crimes was full when the great Reformation caused the downfall of many and the reform of the rest.

"There are still numerous convents existing in Europe, and in America, their number is on the increase. The modern reformer, the socialist and materialist, looks upon them with an evil eye; but the unprejudiced observer won't deny that some of them are doing a great deal of good in their own way. Some have established schools, others opened hospitals, and above all are, the Sisters of Charity unsurpassed in their usefulness in the care of the sick. Thus some of these orders serve the noble purpose of benefiting humanity, and their usefulness could be increased a thousandfold if the light of spiritual knowledge — the Holy Ghost, to whom they pray — were to be permitted to descend upon their ranks.

"Do the religious orders — as they are now — fulfil their original purpose of raising people up into a higher and spiritual state of existence, or are they merely centres around which pious and benevolent people have collected who teach schools and nurse the sick — occupations which might perhaps equally well be performed without professing any particular creed? If the religious convents are calculated to develop true spirituality and to produce truly regenerated men and women, they will be the places where we may find some manifestation of spiritual powers; for a latent power which never manifests itself is of no use; it cannot exist in an active state without manifesting itself. Let us, therefore, be permitted to ask: Do the inhabitants of our convents consciously exercise any spiritual powers? Can they knowingly cure the sick by the touch of their hands? Are their inner senses sufficiently opened so that they may see and hear, taste, smell, and feel things imperceptible to the senses of the average human being? Can they prophesy, with any degree of certainty, future events except by the conclusions of logic? Are there any among them who have become Adepts? What do they know about the conditions required to enter a higher state of consciousness than that of ordinary mortals? What do they know about the means to enter Adeptship and to obtain a conscious future existence? What do our monks and nuns know about the constitution of the human soul, especially those souls entrusted to their care? What are their experiences when in that higher state called *ecstasy*? If one of them enters into a state of trance, is levitated into the air, or produces a simple mediumistic phenomenon, do they know the occult causes which produce such effects? Or is not such an occurrence considered to be an unexplainable or supernatural miracle? Is not the person to whom such a thing happens considered a saint?

"It is idle for the priests to assert that they can forgive sins or that sins can be forgiven through them, for such an assertion can neither be proved nor disproved intellectually: it will always remain a mere matter of opinion. If they don't possess any spiritual powers, we can't believe that they can communicate them to others; and if they convey such powers to others, where are their effects to be seen? Do the ignorant become wise after having been baptized with water? Do those who have submitted to the ceremony of confirmation obtain true faith? Does the sinner become innocent after having the load removed from their conscience through absolution? Can our clergy change the laws of Nature? Can they, by any external ceremony, cause the growth of an inner principle? Or do those who enter a church an animal come out an animal still?

"These are perplexing questions, and I wouldn't like to be understood as if I desired to throw any discredit upon the motives of any of the inhabitants of our convents and nunneries. I am personally acquainted with many of them, and I usually found them to be good and kind and well-meaning people, without that priestly pride and arrogance which unfortunately often characterize the clergy of the world. But I believe that all the good which they do, they could perform as well, and even a great deal better if they were to undertake the study of the soul, its organization and functions, and if they were qualifying themselves for that study. They would then be able to develop consciously those higher faculties which have spontaneously developed among some of their members, who, on account of such an unexpected and abnormal development, were called miracle-workers or saints.

"How can anyone be a true spiritual guide who has no spiritual powers and who, perhaps, doesn't even know that such powers exist? What would you think of a surgeon who knew nothing of anatomy? What of a physician who didn't know their patient? What of a blind painter, a deaf musician, an imbecile mathematician? What shall we think of a physician of the soul who knows nothing about the soul or its attributes, who has never seen it, and is of the mere opinion that it exists? Have we not a right to doubt the usefulness of such a physician and exclaim with Shakespeare: 'Throw physic to the dogs; I'll none of it'?

"If the inhabitants of our convents and monasteries, instead of employing the time and energy which they need for the performance of their customary ceremonies, for the saying of rosaries and the repetitions of litanies, etc., were to employ them to acquire self-knowledge, for the study of the essential constitution of humans and of Nature, and for the acquisition of spiritual power, their usefulness might be extended to an enormous degree. Their knowledge would be no longer restricted to earthly things but expand to heaven; they wouldn't need to nurse the sick, for they could cure them by the touch of their hands. They wouldn't need to baptize people with water, for they could baptize them with the spirit of sanctity; they wouldn't need to listen to confessions, for they would be able to read the thoughts of the culprit. Why should they not be able to do their duties much better if they were wise instead of ignorant; if they knew the truth instead of blindly accepting a creed; if they had the power to accomplish that which they now expect an invisible and unknown power to accomplish in response to their prayers? If the public believes there is one miracle-working saint at a convent, do they not rush there to receive their blessings? What would be the fame of a convent composed entirely of saints whose powers couldn't be doubted?

"But how can monks and nuns acquire such powers? How can they qualify themselves for such a study? It has been said that it is ten times more difficult to remove an old error than to find a new facet of truth, and there lies the difficulty. A page full of writing will have to be cleaned before it can be written on again. They would have to purge their minds of all dogmatism and sophistry before they could see the light of truth; they would have to become like children before they could enter the Kingdom of Heaven within their own souls. They would have to remove the mountain of rubbish which has accumulated in time in the vestibule of the temple, consisting of errors and superstitions, and of

the corpses of forms from which the spirit has fled. Ages of ignorance have contributed to its growth, becoming venerable by age.
The convent's inhabitants bare their heads and bend their knees
when approaching that pile, and they don't dare to destroy it. To
become wise, they would have to learn the true meaning of their
own doctrines, symbols, and books, of which they merely know
the outward form and the dead letter. They would have to form a
much higher and nobler conception of God than to invest Him
with the attributes of a semi-animal human. They would have to
base their moral doctrines upon the intrinsic dignity of the divine
principle in humanity instead of appealing to its selfish desires and
fear of punishment to induce them to seek salvation.

"This may be accomplished in the far-distant future, but not at
the present time. Ages and centuries may roll away before the sunlight of truth will penetrate through the thick veil of materialism
and superstition, which, like an icy crust, covers the true foundation of human religions. Look at the ice fields of the Alps, covering
the sides of the mountains, sometimes many miles in area. They
extend in solid blocks, perhaps more than a hundred feet thick,
down the valley. They are the products of centuries and firm as the
rock the ice appears, and yet these rigid and apparently immovable
masses move and slowly change from year to year. They grate the
rocks upon which they rest, and they throw out that which is foreign. There may be cracks and fissures at the top, and if, as happens
sometimes, someone falls into one of these fissures, their remains
may be found many years afterwards at the foot of the glacier, below the field of ice, having been spewed out by the same.

"Change, slow change, is going on everywhere in Nature. Even
in the most rigid and orthodox religious systems, in the most be-
nighted hearts and heads, there is going on a continual change.
Already the doctrines which were expounded in the pulpits of the
Middle Ages have been modified to a certain extent. The propor-
tions of the devil have shrunk so much that the people have almost
ceased to fear him, and in the same degree as clerical power has
diminished, the conception of God has assumed a grander aspect.
Already the necessity of performing humanitarian labours has

been more fully recognized and is by some considered to be of almost equal importance to the performance of the prescribed ceremonies. Still, the change goes on, gradually but slowly, for there is a powerful giant who, by their negation, resists the decay of the pile of rubbish, and the name of this giant is *Fashion*. It is fashionable to support certain things, so the masses support them.

"Is the progressive part of the world going to wait until the legally appointed guardians of the truth have discovered the value of the treasure in their possession? Have we to wait until they have cleaned the jewel from the dark crust that they have permitted to accumulate around it for centuries? Messengers have arrived from the East, the land of light, where the sun of wisdom has risen, bringing costly moonlight pearls and treasures of liquid gold. Will their untold wealth be entrusted to the safe keeping of those who possess the old and empty forms, or will the new wine be filled in new casks, because the old ones are rotten?

"But why should those who have begun to see the dawn of the day close their eyes and wait until the blind would inform them that the sun is rising over the mountains? Is the love of the truth not strong enough to accomplish what the fear of a dread hereafter has been able to accomplish? Can't the enlightened classes establish academies which would offer all the advantages of orthodox convents without their disadvantages? Couldn't they establish a garden where the divine lotus flower of wisdom might grow and unfold its leaves, sheltered against the storms of passion raging beyond the walls, watered by the water of truth, whose spring is within; where the Tree of Life could unfold without becoming encumbered by the weeds of superstitions and errors; where the soul could breathe the pure spiritual air, unadulterated by the odour of the poison-tree of ignorance, unmixed with the effluvia of decaying superstitions; a place where this Tree of Life, springing from the roots of the Tree of Knowledge, could grow and spread its branches, far up in the invisible realm where Wisdom resides, and produce fruits which cause those who partake of them to become like God and immortal?"

Here the Adept paused as if in deep meditation. But after a moment of silence, he said: "Yes, by all means, establish your theosophical monastery, if you can find any inhabitants duly prepared to enter it; for it will be easier to introduce the truth into a house which is not occupied, than into one which is occupied by its enemies."

"But," I said, "such an institution would require an Adept as a teacher. Would you consent to teach?"

Theodorus answered: "Wherever there is a want, the supply won't fail to come, for *there is no vacuum in Nature.*"

IX

A MAGICAL JOURNEY

t this moment, I heard the sound of the invisible silver bell in the air again, and the Adept, rising, said that he was called away for a few minutes and invited me to remain until he returned. He left the laboratory, and I remained alone. I amused myself by looking over the book containing the *Secret Symbols of the Rosicrucians*. My attention was attracted by the sign of a *Pentagram* turned upside down so that the two points of the lower triangles pointed upwards. Suddenly a voice sounded behind my chair: "In this symbol is contained eternity and time, god and human, angel and devil, heaven and hell, the old and the new Jerusalem with all its inhabitants and creatures."

I turned, and I saw a man by my side with an extremely intelligent face dressed in the habit of a monk. He excused himself for causing an interruption in my thoughts and said that I seemed so deeply engaged in meditating over those figures that I hadn't observed his entrance.

The open countenance, the pleasant looks, and the intelligent expression of my visitor's face at once gained my confidence, and I asked him who he was with whom I had the honour to speak.

"I am," said the stranger, "the *famulus*, or, as you well may call it, the disciple of Theodorus. They call me jocularly his intellectual principle because I have to do his work when the old gentleman is asleep."

I found his remark funny and answered jocularly: "If you are called his intellectual principle, you are perhaps only a creation of his thought. I have seen so many strange things in this place that I wouldn't be surprised by anything. Not even if you were to vanish before my eyes or turn into a snake or a devil."

To this, the apparition replied: "As far as our external appearance is concerned, we are all forms produced by thought, and it is the privilege of beings of a higher order to assume whatever form they find convenient for their purpose. Thus it may sometimes happen that the very devil appears as a saint to delude some gullible fool. I know of cases where some 'jolly spirits' of Nature have assumed the shapes of Christ and the apostles to amuse themselves by misleading some ignoramus. They usually succeed in such cases, but I am neither a devil nor an elemental spirit, and you are neither an ignoramus nor a fool."

I was highly flattered by the favourable opinion expressed by my visitor, and I didn't wish to appear suspicious and thus weaken his faith regarding my power to judge a person's character at first sight. Moreover, he had such a look of benevolence that I didn't wish to distrust him. I, therefore, made him my bow and said: "I haven't the least doubt about your honourable intentions and am quite sure that you are a reliable guide."

"One can't be careful enough in selecting one's guides," continued the stranger. "There are at present so many false prophets and guides. All the world is at present crazy for poking their noses into the mysteries of the astral world. Everybody wants to be taught witchcraft and sorcery. Secrets, which for thousands of years have been wisely kept hidden before the eyes of the unripe and profane, are now bawled out from the housetops and sold at the marketplace as objects of trade. Hundreds of self-appointed 'masters' and guides speculate upon the selfishness and ambitions of their disciples, and, the blind leading the blind, they both come to grief. If only all the seekers for truth were like you, they would not be deluded by false promises held out to them for attaining Adeptship."

"I am really glad," I answered, "that you have discovered my purity and unselfishness of purpose, and I hope that, in consideration of my merits, you will be kind enough to show me some more of your occult secrets. Theodorus has already revealed much wisdom to me, and I listened to him with great interest. But now I want to see something substantial and, if possible, learn how to perform some occult feats."

"Most willingly," said my companion. "I will do all I can for you because you deserve by your unselfishness the patronage of all the Adepts."

So saying, he began to show me some of the curiosities of the laboratory, which contained many strange things. Of some of those I had read in books on alchemy, others were entirely new to me. At last, we came to a closed shrine, and my curiosity led me to ask what it contained.

"Oh!" answered the monk, "this shrine contains some powders for fumigations, by the aid of which you may see the elemental spirits of Nature."

"Indeed!" I exclaimed. "Oh, how I should like to see these lovely spirits! I have read a great deal about them in the books of Paracelsus, but I never had an opportunity of seeing them."

"Not all of them are lovely," said the monk. "The Elementals of Earth have human forms. They are small, but they have the power to elongate their bodies. These gnomes and pigmies are usually ill-humoured and cross, and it is just as well to leave them alone, although sometimes they become very good friends of humans and may even show them hidden treasures and mines. The Elementals of Air, the sylvans, are of a more agreeable nature; still, we cannot rely upon their friendship. The salamanders, living in the element of Fire, are unpredictable, and it is better to have nothing to do with them. But the nymphs and undines are lovely creatures, and they often associate with humans."

"I wish I could see those beautiful water sprites," I said, "but I am inclined to believe that they belong to the realm of the fable. For many years, accounts given by seafarers spoke of mermen and mermaids, which they insisted on having seen at a distance. They said those people were like human beings, of whom the upper part resembled a man or a woman, while the lower part of their body was a fish. They told great stories about their beauty, their waving hair, and how finely they could sing, and they called them sirens because it was said they could sing so well that those who heard their voices would become oblivious of everything else but their songs. At last, such a siren was caught; and it proved to be nothing else than a curious mammal of the species called the *dugong*, which at a distance may be mistaken for a human on account of its colour, and which barks somewhat like a dog. Perhaps those undines and nymphs are also nothing but sea animals."

"This is a most erroneous opinion," answered the monk. "The dugong is an animal, but the nymphs and undines are elemental

spirits of Nature, living in the element of Water, being, under ordinary circumstances, invisible to humans and not being able, to
be caught in this manner. They are almost like human beings but
far more ethereal and beautiful, and under certain circumstances,
they may be seen. They may even attain a permanent material form
and remain on the land. A case is even known in which a certain
Count Stauffenberg married such a nymph because of her beauty
and lived with her for more than a year until some stupid theolo-
gian frightened him by telling him that his wife was a devil. The
count at that time had fallen in love with some good-looking local
girl, and so the interference of the preacher was welcome, and he
took this as a pretext to drive his true wife away. But she revenged
herself, and on the third day after his second marriage, the count
was found dead in his bed. These nymphs are very beautiful. They
are strong in love and are constant, but they are also said to be
very jealous."

The more the monk spoke about the water nymphs, the stronger my desire grew to see them. I asked him to make fumigation
with the mysterious powder. At last, he consented. Putting a few
pieces of dry maple tree bark and some dried leaves of laurel into a
brazier, he added pieces of charcoal and lighted them. He strewed
some of the mysterious powder, and a cloud of white smoke rose,
filling the room like a mist and with a very sweet odour. The objects
in the laboratory could soon only be seen dimly through the mist
and finally disappeared. The walls of the chamber were no more
to be seen.

The air seemed to take on a vibratory motion and to become
denser, but, far from feeling oppressed by this, I felt great exhilaration and satisfaction. At last, I knew I was in the element of
water and was supported by it. I was swimming, but my body was
as light as a feather, and it required no effort whatever to keep me
from sinking; it seemed as if the water was my own element, as if
I were born in it. A light shone directly above my head. I rose up
to the surface and looked around. I was in the midst of the ocean,
dancing up and down with the waves. It was a bright moonlight
night. Above me, the full moon threw its silvery rays upon the

water, causing the ripples and the foamy crests on the tops of the waves to sparkle like liquid silver or diamonds. Far in the distance appeared the coast with a mountain range, which seemed familiar to me. At last, I recognized it as the coast of Sri Lanka, with the range of mountains beyond Colombo and Galle; surely, I couldn't mistake, for I recognized Adam's Peak.

Never shall I forget the agreeable sensation caused by that ethereal bath in the moonlit sea in the Indian Ocean. It seemed to me that, at last, my wish had been fulfilled and that I was free of my mortal body and its weight, yet I was myself. I could see no difference between the body I inhabited now and the one I inhabited before the fumigation. Only my present body was so light that it seemed as if it would float in the air as easily as it did upon the water.

Listen! Some faint sound is brought by the breeze; it seems to be a human voice. It comes nearer, and now I hear it plainly; it is the melodious song of a female voice. I look in the direction from which the sound seems to come, and I see three forms floating upon the waves, rising and sinking and coming nearer. They seem to play with each other, and as they approach, I behold three beautiful "females" with long, wavy hair; but the one in the middle surpasses the others in beauty. She seems to be the queen, for she wears a wreath of water plants upon her head. Still nearer they come. Now they see me and stop. They consult together, but curiosity conquers their fear. They come quite close and speak to me. Their voices are full and melodious; their language is foreign to me, yet I understand what they say. Having discovered that I am a mortal, they appear as anxious to cultivate my acquaintance as I am to be on friendly terms with them.

They invite me to go with them to their home. They speak of their palace constructed of beautiful shells among the coral reefs in the depths of the ocean; of the milk-white pearls with which they have ornamented the walls; of the azure blue of the waves shining through the transparent walls of their houses; and the curious things which no mortal had ever seen. I object and tell them I am mortal and couldn't live in their own element. But the beautiful queen, rising out of the water up to her waist, smiles and shakes her charming head, and fluid diamonds seem to stream from her waving locks. "Come," she whispers, "no harm will befall you, for my servants shall protect you." She extends her beautifully shaped arms towards me and touches my shoulder, and at her touch, my consciousness fades away. I feel that I am dissolving in the element of water. I only dimly hear the distant thunder of the breakers as they roll upon the sandy beach. A moment, and I know nothing more.

X

THE END

J have a little more to add to my tale. I awoke and, opening my eyes, found myself stretched upon the moss in the shadow of that mighty pine, where I had evidently fallen asleep. The sun stood still, high above the western horizon, and far up in the sky, two vultures described long drawn spirals in the air. In their cries, I seemed to recognize the voice of the queen of the nymphs. On the opposite side of the valley was still the rushing waterfall with the foaming basin, and the spray still rose in the air, and the water still flew over the moss-covered edge.

"Has all I have seen been nothing else than a dream?" I exclaimed. "Has that which seemed so beautiful and real been merely an illusion of my brain, and have I now returned to real life?"

I rose, and, as I rose, my eye fell upon the bud of a white lily sticking in a buttonhole of my coat. I couldn't believe my eyes and suspected I was again the victim of a hallucination. I grasped the lily. It didn't vanish; it was as real as the earth upon which I stood. It was of a kind which doesn't grow in these cold mountainous regions; it only grows where the air is mild and warm. I remembered the gold. I put my hand into my pocket, and there, among the few remaining silver pieces, I found a solid lump of gold as bright as the purest; but the little ruby pearls had dropped off from its surface and were lost. I then recollected the precious book the Adept had promised to send me at the village inn. Still, somehow it seemed to me that I had committed an indiscretion during the absence of Theodorus by prying into the secrets of his laboratory and listening to the temptations of the *famulus*. I felt I didn't deserve the favour and was doubtful whether or not he would send me the book.

I flew rather than walked down the mountain, along the road towards the village. Little did I now care for the scenery or the mountaintops, gilded by the rays of the setting sun, or the murmuring river. It grew dark, and the full moon rose over the hills, looking exactly like the moon I had seen some hours before in the Indian Ocean. I calculated the difference in time between Germany and Sri Lanka, and I found that, indeed, I might have seen the moon shine in the Bay of Bengal while the sun was shining in the Alps.

I arrived at O., little heeding the astonished looks of the villagers, who may have believed me insane as I hurried through the streets. I entered the inn, rushed upstairs to my room, and, as I entered, I saw upon the table the precious book, *The Secret Symbols of the Rosicrucians of the Sixteenth and Seventeenth Centuries.* On the flyleaf were written a few lines in pencil, saying:

> *Friend, study this book practically; bring the circle into a square. Mortify the metals; calcinate and purify them of all residua. When you have succeeded, we shall meet again. I shall be with you when you need me.*
>
> *Yours fraternally,*
> *Theodorus*

It may be imagined that, despite my fatigue, I didn't go to sleep very early. I walked up and down in my room, thinking over the events of that memorable day. I tried to find the line between the visible and the invisible, between the objective and subjective, and between dreams and reality. I found that there was no line but that all these terms are merely relative, referring not merely to the conditions of things which appear objective or subjective to ourselves but to our own conditions, and that while in one state of existence, certain things may appear real to us and others elusive. In contrast, in another state, the illusions become real, and that which before seemed to be real is now merely a dream. Perhaps our whole terrestrial life will seem to be at the end, nothing else than a hallucination.

As I walked about the room, I observed a Bible belonging to my host lying in a cupboard. I felt an impulse to open it randomly and see what it said. I did so, and my eye fell upon the twelfth chapter of the second epistle of the Apostle Paul, written to the Corinthians, where it said:

> *I knew a man in Christ, above fourteen years ago (whether in the body or whether out of the body I cannot tell; God knoweth); such a one was caught up into paradise and heard unspeakable words, which it is not lawful for a man to utter.*

H. P. Blavatsky

THANK YOU!

*I*f you have enjoyed *The Land of the Gods*, help other people discover this book by writing a review or just leaving a rating wherever you bought it. This might take only a few minutes, yet it will make a huge difference in bringing this work to the attention of other readers.

You may also take a photo of yourself holding the book and share the news of discovering Madame Blavatsky's long-hidden story on social media with the following hashtags:

#BlavatskyReturns and **#SacredWisdomRevived**

Thank you so much for your help in spreading the word about this book!

If you would like to be informed about our new releases, please sign up for our newsletter at:

radiantbooks.co/bonus

GLOSSARY

ADEPT — one who has attained true knowledge and mastered the Laws of Spirit and Matter, reaching the stages of Initiation and thus becoming a Master of Esoteric Philosophy.

AKASHA (*Sanskrit*, "sky") — Primeval Matter, also known as *Materia Matrix*; the refined, supersensible spiritual essence which pervades all space; primary cosmic substance.

The Akashic Records are a particular manifestation of the limitless and indestructible memory of Nature, which stores information about all events and manifestations of the Cosmos — people, planet, system, or anything else.

BO-TREE or **BODHI TREE** (*Sanskrit*, "tree of awakening") — a large sacred fig tree located in Bodh Gaya, India, under which the Buddha attained enlightenment.

BRAHMA (*Sanskrit*) — the first person of the Hindu Trinity (Trimurti) consisting of Brahma, Vishnu, and Shiva; a hypostasis of the Planetary Spirit; the Creator of the world.

BROTHERHOOD — the Community of the Seven Messengers of the Distant Worlds and their disciples, who have lived side by side with humanity on the Earth for millions of years, developing the human mind and heart. This Brotherhood is usually called *White* to indicate the White Light that, upon splitting, yields the seven colours of the rainbow, each of which symbolizes one of the Great Teachers, and vice versa — the seven colours of the rainbow result in the White Light after their fusion.

The previous Solar System was tasked with giving people knowledge and developing their intelligence. The present System aims to bring people closer to Love, and the focus of Love is the Heart. Therefore, the Great Lords have divided themselves into two Lodges — the Western and the Eastern.

The Western Lodge — also known as the Brotherhood of Luxor or the Thebes Sanctuary, located in Egypt — was to provide knowledge, as well as to develop and expand people's consciousness, with an emphasis on the mental body, the mind, the human intellect, to help take a step towards the heart. All the knowledge accumulated in the past and present Solar Systems resides exclusively in Egypt.

The Eastern Lodge — Shambhala or the Himalayan Brotherhood — was to develop the intuition of the heart, always bearing Love and serving the highest energies. In other words, the West is the mind, and the East is the heart. We learn from ancient traditions that the Masters left the West for the East. Many people, in fact, left the Sanctuary in Egypt to go to the East. This happens approximately once every two thousand years.

At the end of the 19th century, all the Secret Schools and Ashrams of the Western Brotherhood were closed and moved to the Himalayas. All the Great Teachers who had worked in the world — holding Initiations and imparting knowledge — were also summoned to the Stronghold of Light in the Himalayas. Humanity was abandoned for a hundred years, but knowledge was still passed on through their disciples. However, there was no longer any direct contact between the Masters and the vast majority of people.

The Theban Sanctuary is now reopening and once again starting to serve Love. While previously it was working through the Ray of Knowledge, now these two Sanctuaries — the Eastern and the Western — are uniting and interpenetrating their Rays, imparting a single Ray of Love-Wisdom. Similarly, all the Great Lords who had saturated humanity as much as possible with knowledge are now beginning to serve Love. Thus a Great Synthesis is being born, and the two Greatest Schools are merging into one, affirming a single path for the whole world: the ascent to the steps of Wisdom through the illumination of the human heart.

ELEMENTALS — the spirits of the elements of Earth, Water, Air, and Fire (such as genies, elves, undines, dwarfs, etc.).

FAMULUS (*Latin*, "servant") — a disciple.

GOD — the Divine, Unchangeable, Invariable, and Infinite Principle; the eternally Unknowable Cause of All that exists; omnipresent, all-pervading, visible and invisible spiritual Nature, which exists everywhere, in which everything lives, moves, and has its being; the Absolute, including the potential of all things as well as all universal manifestations. Upon being made manifest, out of its Absolute Oneness, God becomes the Absolute of infinite differentiation and its consequences — relativity and opposites. God has no gender and cannot be imagined as a human being. In the Holy Scriptures, God is Fire, God is Love — the one primeval energy that conceives the worlds.

The traditional Christian concept of *God* refers to the Planetary Spirit, or a *Demiurge* (*Greek*, "creator") — the Supreme Lord or Ruler of Earth, who has passed His human evolution and reached an incredibly high level of spiritual development. Together with other High Spirits constituting the Hierarchy of Light, He is now responsible for the creation, preservation, and transfiguration of the Earth.

The Planetary Spirit is androgynous because on the higher planes of Existence, there is no gender separation — hence, the pronoun *He* is used merely for lack of a more appropriate one. The Planetary Spirit can manifest Himself in various Aspects and Hypostases, including male and female in the binary world since He bears within Himself both Principles.

As a rule, the governing Hierarchy of Light for young planets, such as the Earth, consists of High Spirits that came from Distant Worlds, wherein they long ago had gone through the given planet's stage of Evolution. When the humankind of such a planet reaches spiritual maturity, the Lords of Light who arrived from other Worlds leave it, to be replaced by worthy High Spirits who have already gone through their evolution on that young planet.

From ancient sacred texts, it is evident that the Planetary Spirit of the Earth is the Lord of Sirius. Besides, even the Quran states that Allah is the Lord of Sirius. However, it should be borne in mind that the God described in the Old Testament is not the Supreme Lord of the Earth whom Christ calls His Father in the New Testament.

Sometimes He whom we denote by the Name of *the One and Only*, forms simultaneously several of His own Hypostases, as well as Individualities (under different names), and one that possesses a higher energy component serves for another (it may even be said, for Himself) as a Master, Teacher, and Protector — either in the physical world or in the Ethereal, depending on the single Goal which is set before His "emanating forms."

The Nativity Mystery of the Stellar Spirit of Sirius in the Glorious Body on the Higher Planes of the Earth occurred for the first time on the planet on 19 July 2017. It is significant not only for the Earth and the Solar System but also for all the constellations headed and supervised by Sirius. This Mystery of Light will never be repeated in the present Grand Cycle of Evolution.

GODS — the Spirits of the Higher Spheres, Distant Worlds, who have achieved a high level of evolution, far surpassing the earthly humanity that led people to begin perceiving them as Gods. In other words, this level of spiritual achievement is also destined for humanity.

In Tibet, such a Spirit is called by the ancient word *Lha* (*Tibetan*, "Spirit," "God"), which covers the entire series of celestial Hierarchies. Every Supreme Concept of the Cosmos is personified in a High Spirit that also takes a human form. That is why every ancient religion has a pantheon of Gods, each of whom embodies a certain Idea and represents a particular Force of Nature.

The Sons of God, the Sons of Light, the Sons of Heaven, the Sons of Fire, the Sons of Reason, the Archangels, the Regents of Planets, the Masters of Wisdom, the Bodhisattvas (*Sanskrit*, "Enlightenment Beings"), the Dhyan Chohans (*Sanskrit*, "Lords of Light"), the Rishis (*Sanskrit*, "Sages of Insight"), the Kumaras (*Sanskrit*, "Youths"), and so on — these are High Spirits, who, like the Avatars, assumed a human appearance to raise the consciousness of humanity and accelerate its development. The Seven

Great Spirits have taken care of the planet Earth and its humanity. Again and again, they were incarnated as the greatest founders of kingdoms, religions, sciences, and philosophies to help people unite with their divine nature. And so they have left deep traces in every domain of life and in every land.

For example, among their incarnations on the Earth are Akbar the Great, Anaxagoras, Apollonius of Tyana, Confucius, the Count of Saint-Germain, Francis of Assisi, Gautama Buddha, Giordano Bruno, Hermes Trismegistus, Jakob Böhme, Jesus Christ, John the Apostle, Joseph, Joshua, King Arthur, Krishna, Lao-Tzu, Mahatma Koot Hoomi, Mahatma Morya, Melchizedek, Menes, Moses, Muhammad, Numa Pompilius, Origen, Orpheus, Paul the Apostle, Pericles, Plato, Pythagoras, Rama, Ramesses the Great, Sergius of Radonezh, Solomon, Thomas à Kempis, Thutmose III, Tsongkhapa, Tutankhamun, Zoroaster, and many others.

All the Gods have their Spouses, who in the Higher Worlds are united, and one does not exist without the other. But, since the Masculine Principle must express itself in the visible aspect of life and the Feminine Principle in the invisible, the Female Deities were revered as the most sacred and secret in all ancient religions. It is they — who have been incarnated on the Earth as mothers, sisters, daughters, and wives — through self-sacrifice, heroism, and continuous giving, inspired the Sons of Light and the peoples of the Earth, as well as humanity as a whole. Similarly, the entire Hierarchy of Light devoutly honours the Mother of the World — the Great Spirit of the Feminine Principle, who has Her personifications in many world religions as the Supreme Goddess. The Mother of the World incarnated Herself as Mary to give life to Jesus Christ. After that, for the past two thousand years, she has manifested Herself through Her Hypostasis-Daughters — Faith, Hope, and Love, who have continuously replaced each other and have never abandoned this world.

KABBALAH (*Hebrew*, "tradition") — the ancient Chaldean Secret Doctrine and an occult system handed down by oral transmission. Once, it was the fundamental science of cosmogony but has been distorted by centuries-old accretions and interpolations of western occultists, especially the Christian mystics.

The modern Kabbalah represents a mystic current in Judaism that emerged in the Middle Ages. It deals with esoteric interpretations of the Hebrew Scriptures and teaches several methods of interpreting Biblical allegories.

KARMA (*Sanskrit*, "action") — the Cosmic Law of Cause and Effect, which is expressed in the formula, "as you sow, so shall you reap"; defines the frames within which the destiny of an individual, people, planet, and so on can be developed.

Karma neither punishes nor rewards; it is simply a single Universal Law that infallibly guides all other laws, producing certain effects in accordance with corresponding causes. Every word, action, thought, or desire leads to an appropriate effect — and, eventually, to everything in one's surroundings. Nothing happens accidentally. Karma may be individual and collective, embracing whole peoples, continents, planets, and star systems. One cannot change or eliminate it except by removing the causes underlying human actions.

Everyone bears the mark of karmic predestination right from birth. And their free will is limited by the frames determined by Karma, which is created by their own human will. However, the placing of obstacles and restrictions in one direction opens opportunities in another. The purpose of Karma is to direct everyone towards the path of Evolution. Hence Love is the quickest way of redeeming one's Karma.

LOGOS (*Greek*, "word") — the manifested Deity; the outward expression, or effect, of the cause which is ever concealed.

MASTERS OF WISDOM — the Great Teachers, the Lords of Shambhala, the Sons of the Only Begotten God, the Mahatmas, the Seven Instructors of Humanity, who have taken responsibility for its evolution. Through suffering and sacrifice, they have achieved a high level of development, far surpassing that of ordinary people — and, of course, to human understanding, they can be seen as Gods. In the 19th and early 20th centuries, six Mahatmas were incarnated, known under these names: Morya, Koot Hoomi, Saint-Germain, Serapis, Hilarion, and Djual Khool. Now they are no longer in their former bodies, and they have also changed their names; some have gone to other, more advanced planets, leaving worthy earthly successors in their place.

The Masters are the Great Guardians of Truth, who implement the Divine Plan. They know when, what, and how much should be given to people and attentively watch over their evolution. There is so much intense work that the Mahatmas have no time for anything personal. They create new causes that bring about the effects needed for Evolution — thereby helping humanity to liquidate its former Karma. They know in advance the course of consequences and can project them for millennia ahead. And sometimes, when the Teachers foresee the future, they simply know the effects of the causes consciously produced by them. So, they create the future, which is pliant in the hands of their fiery will. The Masters know the course of the stars and their future combinations and coordinate their creative work with the energies of the Cosmos.

One of the most essential tasks of the Great Brotherhood is the selection and guidance of colleagues and disciples. For various reasons, the Teachers cannot enter into direct and close contact with multitudes of people. But they act through their colleagues, disciples, and messengers. When their disciples are incarnated on Earth with a definite mission, the Masters follow and guide them right from childhood. The karmic relationship of long millennia enables the Instructors to make contact with their disciples without difficulty. In addition to being taught secret sciences, they usually undergo a fiery transmutation that allows them to maintain communication with the Masters. The disciples are constantly on probation, even at higher levels of development. The most terrible betrayals are also unavoidable in their lives.

Each century, the Mahatmas admit into the Abode of Light a maximum of two candidates to convey through them a part of the Secret Knowledge. But this may not always be necessary for various reasons. The chief consideration is that the messenger's body must be ready to receive the Teaching. The Teachings of Light, of course, never appear spontaneously — there are specific periods allotted to them. To record them, the disciples go through many incarnations of preparation and probation, sometimes for thousands of years, and when the time comes, they are warned about the work they are about to undertake. As a rule, preliminary preparation takes place for three years, when the Higher Spirits work with the disciples, getting their bodies in tune.

Contrary to established opinion, the Great Teachers never come into contact with mediums or channellers. Helena Blavatsky had to take the body of a powerful medium, which was necessary for the tasks assigned to her during her final life on Earth. She had to work with many people and perform miracles to convince them of the existence of the higher Laws of Nature and Supreme Knowledge. Nevertheless, with the help of her Master, she brought her ability under complete control. Before revealing *The Secret Doctrine* to humanity, Blavatsky had been undergoing the fiery transmutation of her body for three years under the supervision of her Teacher in one of His Ashrams in Tibet. For those who have endured this process, it is tough to be out amongst people, and all the more so amongst those adversely disposed against them. This is why Blavatsky had such poor health. The situation was similar with Helena Roerich, but it was even more intense when she received *Agni Yoga*. However, she lived in India almost in solitude, being surrounded by loving people and the pure mountain air — which allowed her to almost wholly accomplish the mission of her last earthly incarnation.

Initially, when the Leaders of Humanity came into the world, the continents were divided into seven spheres, wherein each of the Great Lords gave off their own luminous vibrations. As the rainbow is dispersed into seven colours, so all the Seven Great Teachers represent the Seven Rays, bringing with them the currents consonant with their particular note. By the present time, each of the Seven Masters of Wisdom has educated disciples who have reached a high level of consciousness, and the exact number of the Leaders of Humanity is now 777. Certainly, the Teachers have their own Teachers, for cognition is limitless.

In essence, the Seven Great Teachers — the Seven Rays — are the components of the One Supreme Lord, who represents the White Ray and personifies the Spiritual Sun. Thus, there is One Individuality, but His partial manifestations enlightened such earthly incarnations as Buddha, Christ, Maitreya, and other Great Teachers.

NIRVANA (*Sanskrit*, "blown out") — the state of complete enlightenment and liberation, the highest tension and development of all the possibilities inherent in the human body. This state can be achieved during one's lifetime, as evidenced by the lives of all the Saints. Nirvana can also be called the *fiery ascent* because it represents the seventh state of matter, or the Seventh Plane of Existence, which one can reach. This is the only Reality in which neither Time nor Space exists, where one can experience bliss from complete unity with one's Spirit. The rest of the spheres, or planes, represent only various degrees of illusion, where the physical world is the greatest illusion.

OCCULTISM (*Latin*, "hidden," "secret") — the totality of sciences that study spiritual forces in humans and the Cosmos, as well as the incomprehensible properties of matter and consciousness.

PRALAYA (*Sanskrit*, "dissolution") — a period of rest, or collapse of life within a planet, system, galaxy, or the Universe between various Cycles of Evolution. It is equivalent in duration to *Manvantara* (*Sanskrit*, "Age of a Manu") — a period of active life within a planet, system, galaxy, or the Universe.

SHAMBHALA (*Sanskrit*, "Place of Peace") — the Stronghold of Light, a legendary kingdom hidden in the heart of the Himalayas. It is known under different names in the myths and beliefs of various world peoples: Agartha, Belovodye, the City of Gods, the Garden of Eden, Mount Meru, the Pure Land, the White Island,

and so on. Shambhala is the Imperishable Sacred Land, the first and ever-present continent of the planet Earth, which never shared the fate of the others, for it is destined to continue from the beginning to the end of the Grand Cycle of Evolution. It is the cradle of the first human and contains the sacral Source of all religions, philosophies, sciences, and esoteric teachings. This mysterious place, which preserves the Eternal Wisdom, lies at the intersection of the past, present, and future, as well as the Physical, Subtle, and Fiery Worlds.

Shambhala was first mentioned in the Puranas. Information about it filtered into the world at different times. Back in the 10th century, one of the monks of Kievan Rus had been staying in the Ashram of the Great Brotherhood for several days. However, he wasn't allowed to talk about it, except upon his deathbed, to tell his story "from mouth to ear." It was not until 1893, in fact, that this account was written down.[1] In the 12th and 13th centuries, Popes Alexander III and Innocent IV both attempted to establish contact with Prester John, the head of the Secret Spiritual Brotherhood in the heart of Asia, who had sent letters to several Christian sovereigns: Constantine the Great, Manuel I Komnenos, Frederick I Barbarossa, Louis VII of France, and others. In the 17th century, the Portuguese Jesuit missionary, Estêvão Cacella, was the first to tell the Europeans of this mythical place, which he visited at the invitation of the Tibetans. In 1915, Albert Grünwedel published a German translation of the Guidebook to Shambhala, written by the famous Panchen Lama, Lobsang Palden Yeshe, in which the location of this legendary realm is indicated by a mass of symbols and complex geographical hints. And in 1925, in many newspapers worldwide, an extensive article by the Mongolian explorer, Dr. Lao Chin, appeared, telling of his journey to the Valley of Shambhala. He was forbidden to write about the wondrous spiritual phenomena there. However, Dr. Lao Chin mentioned that the valley's inhabitants lived for many centuries but looked like middle-aged people, and they were characterized by clairvoyance,

---

[1] Published in English as *The Kingdom of White Waters* (New York: Radiant Books, 2022).

telepathy, and other higher abilities. Among other things, he saw how they levitated and even became invisible to the physical eye.[1]

Shambhala is the Ashram of the Great Brotherhood of the Teachers of Humanity, each of whom is a God, having become such for many nations and leaving the divine mark in human hearts as an equal among equals in the flesh. The work of the Mahatmas may be seen in three principal directions of research: the improvement of the earthly plane, methods of communication with the Distant Worlds, and means of conveying the results of their study to humanity. The latter is indeed the most challenging of all.

The Shambhala of the Earth may be thought of as a spaceport from which messengers are sent to the Distant Worlds and where ambassadors from the infinite Universe arrive. New ideas from other inhabited planets are tested in the laboratories of the Brotherhood; after being adapted to earthly conditions, they are conveyed to scientists of the world as inspiration.

Here the most important decisions concerning the evolution of humanity and the planet are made. Once every hundred years, the Council of Shambhala is convened (1924, 2024); once every sixty years, the Council of the High Initiates takes place. It is a real World Government, which has little in common with earthly regimes, but still, it has often contacted them through its messengers. Indeed, the history of all times and nations records testimonies to the Assistance of the Great Teachers, which has always been secretly given at turning points in the history of every country. However, while the people of the East often accepted their advice, the West, as a rule, rejected them.

For example, in addition to the aforementioned information, it is known that warnings were received by the representatives of the Habsburg dynasty and the Norwegian King Cnut the Great. Charles XII of Sweden was warned not to start his fatal campaign against Russia. The repeated warnings to Louis XVI and Marie Antoinette of the impending danger to France and the French royal family are widely known. Napoleon was also warned not to

---

[1] If you are interested in reading Dr. Lao Chin's article about his journey to one of the Abodes of Shambhala, please visit radiantbooks.co/bonus.

go against Russia. A warning was given to Queen Victoria in 1851. And in 1926, the Mahatmas issued an austere warning to the government of the USSR, and the consequences of its rejection were indeed grave. Further, an unknown Tibetan lama passed a warning to Hitler through German zoologist Ernst Schäfer that he should not start a "great war."

On the other hand, American Presidents George Washington and Abraham Lincoln listened to the advice of the Great Brotherhood, which resulted in the development of the United States. In the 1930s, however, when President Franklin Roosevelt was warned about the upcoming Second World War, he, unfortunately, didn't take all the advice he was given to heart, or there would be a United States of both Americas today.[1]

Several prominent people also visited Shambhala. As a rule, one or two candidates are admitted there each "century" (which consists not of a hundred years but sixty, according to the Kalachakra Calendar). For example, during their lifetimes, this Stronghold of Light was visited by: Gautama Buddha, Jesus Christ, Lao-Tzu, Pythagoras, Plato, Apollonius of Tyana, Paracelsus, the Panchen Lama Palden Yeshe, Helena Blavatsky, Helena and Nicholas Roerich, and others — all of whom have played a significant role in the evolution of humanity. But not all the Great Spirits who had certain missions to fulfil visited the Brotherhood during their earthly life. Furthermore, anyone who visits this Abode of Light by invitation resonating deeply in their heart takes a vow of silence, which may be broken only with the permission of the Great Lord of Shambhala. An uninvited guest will never find the right way to reach it.

SHIVA (*Sanskrit*, "auspicious one") — the third person of the Hindu Trinity (Trimurti) consisting of Brahma, Vishnu, and Shiva; a hypostasis of the Planetary Spirit. His character of Destroyer is higher than that of Vishnu the Preserver, for He destroys only to regenerate on a higher plane.

[1] See Helena Roerich, *The Secret World Government* (New York: Radiant Books, 2023).

In the current Solar System, the Ray of Shiva — the First Ray of Will and Power — cannot be manifested in full measure since it acquires a destructive aspect if there are not enough loving and pure hearts. To perceive this Ray, one must first assimilate the Ray of Vishnu — the Second Ray of Love-Wisdom. The manifestation of the First Ray in the current Solar System is the Seventh Ray — the Ray of Transfiguration, whose Lord is the Master Rakoczy, also known as Saint-Germain.

VISHNU (*Sanskrit*, "all-pervasive") — the second person of the Hindu Trinity (Trimurti), consisting of Brahma, Vishnu, and Shiva; a hypostasis of the Planetary Spirit that is associated with the Lord M. in Theosophy.

The Messiahs of all peoples and times, such as Rama, Krishna, Zoroaster, Buddha, Christ, and Maitreya, are Avatars or incarnations of Vishnu.

ABOUT THE AUTHOR

ELENA PETROVNA BLAVATSKY (1831–1891) laid the foundation of unity of all religions and philosophies, taking upon herself the most challenging labour of all — sharing with people the Secret Knowledge, which before that time couldn't be so broadly revealed to the world. Under the guidance of the Mahatmas Morya and Koot Hoomi, she synthesized all ancient teachings into two capital works: *Isis Unveiled* and *The Secret Doctrine*. Aimed at the human intellect, Madame Blavatsky's writings were to bring about a fundamental shift in the ossified consciousness of humanity and to enlighten the best minds. Revealing cosmogony and our lost history, *The Secret Doctrine* was significantly ahead of its time. It later allowed outstanding scientists like Thomas Edison, Nikola Tesla, and Albert Einstein to make many scientific discoveries that have changed our world.

WORKS:

- *The Secret Doctrine*
- *Isis Unveiled*
- *The Key to Theosophy*
- *The Voice of the Silence*
- *From the Caves and Jungles of Hindostan*
- *The People of the Blue Mountains*
- *The Durbar in Lahore*
- *Collected Writings*

OTHER TITLES PUBLISHED BY RADIANT BOOKS

THE SECRET WORLD GOVERNMENT
by Helena Roerich

A secret for many years, this book provides the first-ever evidence showing how the Secret World Government, known as *Shambhala*, helped the United States during the Franklin D. Roosevelt presidency. It outlines profound principles for becoming a true leader who can guide any nation to prosperity by building just relations between the people and the state.

THE TEMPLE OF MYSTERIES
by Francia La Due

Bridging spirituality and science, this classic work is a true gem of the world's esoteric legacy. The Master Hilarion, the Protector of America and Europe, transmitted it through Francia La Due, intending to assist humanity in resolving the challenges of modern civilization and guide us toward unity with the cosmic forces that shape our existence. *The Temple of Mysteries* will illuminate your path to self-realization and help you find answers to the most pressing questions that trouble your soul.

THE MYSTERY OF CHRIST
by Thales of Argos

Eye-opening and heart-touching, *The Mystery of Christ* brings a fresh perspective, an uncommon insight, and spiritual depth to the dramatic events which occurred two thousand years ago. As you read the profoundly stirring pages of this beautifully crafted narrative, you will comprehend the unequalled mission of Christ and the innermost secrets of Mary, culminating in an unexpected encounter with the new mystery of the Cosmos named Sophia.

BECOMING WHAT YOU ARE
by Two Workers

Drawing on timeless spiritual wisdom, this book will take you on a journey toward self-realization and inner awakening. Its inspiring messages and practical advice will show you how to cultivate the qualities necessary for spiritual growth. It will help you align your actions with your highest potential and ultimately become what you are — a radiant and awakened being.

THE SEVEN LAWS OF SPIRITUAL PURITY
by Two Workers

Providing a profound and eye-opening perspective on achieving true spiritual purity, this thought-provoking and straightforward book draws practical advice from ancient wisdom to show you how to purify your mind, body, and soul. It is a passionate plea for a better world — a world in which humanity no longer has to accept and deal with the consequences of many sufferings but instead prevents their very causes.

THE KINGDOM OF WHITE WATERS
by V.G.

For a thousand years, this secret story could be told only on the deathbed, for it revealed an inaccessible garden paradise hidden in the Himalayas — Shambhala, a place thousands of people searched for, but always failed to find. Each carrier of this secret story took a vow of silence that could be broken under only two conditions: when facing imminent death or in response to another's persistent requests for knowledge about the mythical Kingdom of White Waters.

Printed in Great Britain
by Amazon

37000258R00088